Mike Hutton is a writer of social history and a novelist. He has a keen interest in early twentieth century British art. He lives with his wife in the heart of England.

Children of the 1940s

This book is dedicated to the memory of the author's parents –
Jack & Doris Hutton

Children of the 1940s

A Social History

Mike Hutton

PEN & SWORD
HISTORY

First published in Great Britain in 2023 by
Pen & Sword History
An imprint of Pen & Sword Books Limited
Yorkshire – Philadelphia

Copyright © Mike Hutton 2023

ISBN 978 1 39904 950 4

The right of Mike Hutton to be identified as
Author of this Work has been asserted by him in accordance
with the Copyright, Designs and Patents Act 1988.

A CIP catalogue record for this book is
available from the British Library

Typeset by Mac Style
Printed in the UK by CPI Group (UK) Ltd, Croydon, CR0 4YY.

Pen & Sword Books Limited incorporates the imprints of After the
Battle, Atlas, Archaeology, Aviation, Discovery, Family History,
Fiction, History, Maritime, Military, Military Classics, Politics,
Select, Transport, True Crime, Air World, Frontline Publishing,
Leo Cooper, Remember When, Seaforth Publishing, The Praetorian
Press, Wharncliffe Local History, Wharncliffe Transport,
Wharncliffe True Crime and White Owl.

For a complete list of Pen & Sword titles please contact

PEN & SWORD BOOKS LIMITED
47 Church Street, Barnsley, South Yorkshire, S70 2AS, England
E-mail: enquiries@pen-and-sword.co.uk
Website: www.pen-and-sword.co.uk
or
PEN AND SWORD BOOKS
1950 Lawrence Rd, Havertown, PA 19083, USA
E-mail: Uspen-and-sword@casematepublishers.com
Website: www.penandswordbooks.com

Contents

Acknowledgements

I am indebted to Joan Beretta whose constant help and attention has made this book possible.

My thanks also to the following whose recollections bring a sense of time and reality to a world so different from that of today:

Jean Sporle, Martin van Oppen, Arthur Price-Jones, Albert Knight, Iris Chapple, Gerry Southworth, Raymond Cooney, Sylvia Cooney, Ann Spiers, Jean Clarke, Iris Robinson, Anne Prowse, Ronnie Pitt, Robin Burns, Elizabeth Davies, Terry Norton, Sheila van de Velde, Pat Desbruslais, Peggy Weber, Shirley Balmer, Margaret Woodcock, Michael Goddard.

Photographic acknowledgements

The author is grateful to the following for permission to reproduce the illustrations used in this book:

The Mary Evans Picture Library
Joan Beretta
Ronnie Pitt
Ann Spiers
Anne Cash
Arthur Price-Jones
Jean Frame
Martin van Oppen
Gerry Southworth
Sheila Southworth

Prologue

Recent films and TV series illustrate how difficult it is to recreate life in the 1940s. Small errors jar and irritate. Inappropriate contemporary phraseology features in the dialogue. Worse, despite the research and care taken, the stars still look like actors playing a part. This is largely because the producers, directors and cast are too young and were not alive at the time and are unable to recreate the essence of that far off time.

Children of the 1940s give voice to that generation's account of life eighty years ago. Extraordinary stories never told before. Some desperately sad, others funny and heart warming. A difficult childhood, but one generally looked upon with some affection by this tribe who have now grown old but still remember.

Part I

War Time

Chapter 1

The Bare Facts 1945

'If you carry your childhood with you, you never become older'
Tom Stoppard, born 1937

It was Wendy who suggested that we should all take our clothes off. Wendy was a precocious nine year old, whilst her little friends Alice, Tony, Kit and myself were only seven. Outside the rain continued to pour down as August splashed its way into early September. We were bored. We had spent weeks cycling up to Scratch Woods and Stanmore Common. There we had careered down narrow paths, pretending to be cowboys one day and knights in armour the next. Endless games of football had been completed until the ball got a puncture, and cricket had been curtailed when our leather ball was lost in undergrowth and the substitute bald tennis ball had finally fallen apart.

As we contemplated Wendy's proposal, she informed us that she would soon be growing breasts. Somehow this fact put us boys rather on the back foot. Not to be out-done, Tony informed us that because he was dark haired he would be shaving by the time he was twelve. We all studied Wendy's flat outline and Tony's smooth face. The silence was broken by Tony informing us that we would not be disturbed as his mother had gone to see her sister in Swiss Cottage and would not be back until after tea time. That established, Wendy was as good as her word. Quickly she peeled off her blouse and vest and stood proudly in front of us. Alice, by contrast, took a deal of encouragement before she too was stripped to the waist. Entering into the spirit of things, the boys too were peeling off jumpers and shirts. The whiteness of our skinny bodies were in stark contrast to our sunburnt arms. My shoulder blades protruded like angels' wings. It would have almost been possible to hang a rack of clothes from them. Now came the acid test.

Suddenly Wendy seemed less sure about taking her skirt off. Time for decisive action. Tony dropped his trousers, whilst we untangled braces in an attempt to keep up. The girls giggled as they stared at our nakedness. Ever observant, Wendy declared that Tony's was different. He informed her that he was a roundhead whilst we were cavaliers. His tone suggested that made us inferior in some way. As yet we had no knowledge of the English Civil War, but the definition was clear for all to see. Now it was the girls' turn and soon amidst a haze of blue school knickers, all of us were as naked as the day we were born. There was a real sense of anti-climax.

The girls were like mermaids with legs. For a moment we all stood looking at each other and then, as if controlled by some unseen conductor, we all started dancing. This was no formal waltz or foxtrot, nor even a jive or the jitterbug currently sweeping the country. No, this was as if the casting off of our clothes had released some primeval force. We leapt, arms and legs akimbo, onto armchairs and the settee. We whooped and hollered as if somehow we had been released from convention and it felt exhilarating. It seemed a natural progression as we three boys started wrestling with each other. It was not serious fighting and we were laughing as we fell in a heap on the carpet. As we wriggled and writhed in an attempt to break free, the girls threw themselves on top of us. There was a smell of shampooed hair and young flesh as we cavorted. It must have looked like a scene from a Roman orgy.

Our frolics were cut short by a sharp rap on the window. For a second no one moved, as if by not moving we could avoid the consequences of our action. Whilst the others were now grasping at their pile of clothes and starting to dress, I stood hopelessly staring at the vague outline of Tony's mother at the window. I could just make out through the net curtains her figure dressed in black and wearing that distinctive hat featured in a recurring nightmare I had been experiencing recently. For nights past I had been pursued down the corridor of a train by an old woman dressed in black and wearing a hat with a veil that masked her face. The nightmare always ended with me falling out of bed. Now I was facing a real life nightmare and Mrs. Wilson was now rattling the letter box and shouting ominously. Tony was almost dressed and he was crying. I pulled on my pants and short trousers and made for the kitchen and my route for escape. Leaving Tony to the wrath of his mother, I was further alarmed as I crossed the hall to see a pair of dark angry eyes staring at me through the letter box.

The rain continued to lash down. There was no sign of the other children who had obviously scaled the back garden fence. Pulling on my shirt and throwing my jumper and shoes over the fence, I made to follow them. There was a narrow track of land behind the house which had been due to carry tube trains north from Edgware to Stonegrove, a new station designed to transport the growing army of commuters travelling each day to the West End or the city. The extension had been delayed by the war and was in fact never built. The wooden fence stood some six foot tall. It is astonishing what fear can do, for I clambered over like a frightened monkey and hid in a clump of bushes. I could hear Mrs. Wilson shouting, but she was too small to look over the fence. It was only now that two very important facts hit me. Firstly, my legs were bleeding following my mad scramble over the fence. Worse, I was aware that I had dropped one of my shoes. For a moment I contemplated climbing back to retrieve my shoe, but I realised that the lady in black had probably already found it.

Ducking low, I scampered away from the house. By now I realised I was covered in stings from the nettles that I had not even noticed in my panic. My arms and legs had also been lacerated by brambles. Despite the discomfort and pain, my real worry was how I could explain away my appearance and lost shoe to my mother. As the rain intensified, I tried walking with just one shoe on, but I soon gave that up. Needing time to think, I made my way along the track to what we called the brick fields. The fledgling station had been built to platform level before it was abandoned. We had devised a secret method of scaling the building from ground level. There was one part that had a covered wooden roof which we used as our 'secret den'. At least I was sheltered from the rain as I sat there and gloomily tried to think up an excuse for my appearance. My single shoe stared up at me balefully. I was in big trouble and I knew it. Girls were just trouble and I was already convinced that it was the boys who would get the blame.

Our den was something of a fortress. Several groups of older boys had tried to take it over, but whilst it was difficult to scale the walls there was only one way down and that was to jump. The drop looked huge to a seven year old, although it was probably only about twenty feet. Whilst our young frames generally took the impact on landing well, the older boys often injured themselves and so it was that the six or seven of us who were a group of friends were left to defend our den in peace. It still remained a tricky undertaking. The ascent was made by various bricks having been removed that allowed us scramble up, although the danger of losing our footing and falling back was a constant worry. Having reached platform height, launching yourself down took some nerve. For some one jump was enough and they never returned to what we considered to be our elite group. The weather was an important factor. Earlier in the holiday during a prolonged dry spell, I had sprained my ankle and been banned from returning by my mother. Even now when the ground was sodden you needed to steel yourself for a safe landing. Members of our gang used different techniques. Some would sit on the edge before jumping, whilst others just launched themselves. There was always a moment of exhilaration on landing relatively unscathed. Despite having made numerous jumps, doubts and fear sometimes returned unexpectedly.

It is a strange thing that even as children we often sought solitude to confront problems. I had sat listening to the rain splashing on the wooden roof of our lair trying to think of a good reason for my bedraggled appearance and the loss of a shoe. None came to me and now suddenly I was afraid of making the jump. Several times I stood on the edge before retreating again. Finally plucking up courage I launched myself into space, landing awkwardly and falling into a clump of stinging nettles. As I searched for some dock leaves I realised to my horror I had left my remaining shoe in the den. Leaving it there was not really an option. With shoes rationed, it was the only pair I had and presumably the dreaded Mrs. Wilson would return the other one. Up I clambered again. This time holding the shoe I did not hesitate and landed safely. Now for the walk of shame home. All those twitching curtains as neighbours tracked my progress. I made my way past the allotments into Green Lane. This was an un-adopted road skirted by fields, where today blocks of flats loom and traffic from the A41 provides a constant background of noise. Back in 1945 it was still possible to believe you were in the countryside as our road formed the outward border of the sprawl of suburbia. My fears about twitching curtains had been trumped. The rain had stopped and it appeared half of our neighbours were out in their gardens tracking my progress. I was quizzed on what I had been up to, whilst others offered sympathy for my cuts and bruises. Any hope of me slipping into our house without being noticed was dispelled by the figure of my mother waiting at the front gate. Shaking her head she just said 'bath' and guided me indoors. I do not know what I was expecting, perhaps a furious telling off or the favourite 'you wait until I tell your father', but no, my mother tended my scratches and stings without any questioning about my appearance or loss of my shoe. Perhaps I was going to get away with it after all. Nothing was said either when my father returned. It was too good to last. Just as I was going up to bed my mother informed me in a jolly voice that Mrs. Wilson had rung and that she would be coming to see us in the morning. That night I had no nightmares about a woman dressed in black chasing me down a train corridor because I was now so worried I hardly managed any sleep.

At breakfast the stand-off continued. No mention was made of yesterday's mishaps, although I did notice a conspiratorial glance between my sister and mother. They were using silence to unnerve me. I told them I was going out to ride my bike. Not without shoes I wasn't, I was told and reminded ever so sweetly that Mrs. Wilson would be along shortly. I went to my bedroom which had a good view down the street. This gentle approach to my shocking behaviour was unsettling. The quiet before the storm. Then there she was. A small figure dressed in blue rather than black. Her hat was blue as well. She carried a small handbag and my missing shoe.

My mother and Mrs. Wilson, whilst knowing each other, were not friends, probably because our two houses were about a half mile apart. I went out onto the landing to see if I could hear what was being said. I was shocked to hear laughter rather than voices full of indignation. Actually the laughter became louder. Curiosity led me down the stairs and I could see them now shaking at something that had been said. Turning, they spotted me. Close up, Mrs. Wilson was not the frightening figure of my imagination. She had a kind face. Turning to me she handed me the shoe. 'Yours, I believe.' They moved into the kitchen to have coffee, leaving me feeling uncertain on how to react.

I am not sure that my mum ever told my father about the affair. Certainly he never mentioned it. All my mother ever said about the incident was that Wendy had accused the boys of being the instigators. As I started to protest, she seemed to acknowledge our relative innocence. Wendy had apparently already acquired something of a reputation. However my mother sternly lectured me to always be respectful to young girls. Our little gang decided never to never play with girls again, although 'kiss-chase' in the playground was always fun.

This early memory happened to coincide with the end of the war in Europe. Our generation had experienced far more serious events over the past five years.

Chapter 2

Setting the Scene

Currently it is estimated that there are in excess of three million people living in Great Britain who are over eighty years old. Back in the 1940s they formed an army of skinny children, the boys all baggy shorts and wrinkled socks, whilst the girls are remembered in pigtails or plaits.

Today these youngsters have grown old. They are a tough bunch who have survived a world war and the crippling austerity that followed. They have witnessed the formation of the National Health Service and the huge social changes that are still underway. They partied during the Sixties, fell in love, most getting married although some subsequently enduring a painful divorce. They had children and many now have grandchildren, some even great-grandchildren. Now they are confronted with a world so different from the one they were brought up in, that many feel somewhat bewildered by the speed of change.

Conversely how would the youngsters of today fare if cast back to the 1940s? How would they cope without their iPhones, computers and social media? Worse, there wasn't even any television to distract from the cold they would have felt in winter with no central heating. Virtually no fridges either, so milk had to be kept in buckets of water in summer to stop it curdling. Food was rationed, so you were expected to eat whatever was on the plate or go without. Eating disorders were unheard of as mothers tried to think of innovative ways to fill their children's grumbling stomachs.

Few families had cars and it was normal for children to walk to school, often miles away from home. For many it was a time of absent fathers, most of whom would have been serving in the armed forces. Parents fretted at the real possibility of a German invasion, although children have a unique ability to put worries to the back of their minds as they charge around in the enthusiasm of the moment.

So the children of the 1940s were a different breed from today's youngsters. No better, but different. Many endured the horrors of the bombing of our industrial cities. Of fathers being killed, injured or captured, but at the time they were encouraged just to 'get on with it' no matter how devastating the news. Today doubtless this attitude would be seriously criticised but no one I spoke to while compiling this book can remember any counselling. Boys particularly were expected to be brave whatever the circumstances. Of course people were kind but for the time being the British stiff upper lip was firmly in place.

Back eighty odd years ago there was still a deference towards authority. At school discipline was rigid and unchanging. The class stood up when a teacher entered the room and the cane was still much in evidence. The respect for authority extended to doctors and, of course, policemen who could still be seen daily pounding the beat on the streets of both cities, towns and villages. The deference extended beyond children to adults as rank and social class divisions still persisted despite a gradual erosion. This was most noticeable in rural areas where the local landowner continued to hold sway. He and his family occupied the front pew in the village church each Sunday and those in his employ were expected to troop in behind. The greatest respect was reserved for the Royal Family. Children were brought up to be proud of the country and its empire. The King's faltering Christmas address was listened to attentively despite its normally banal content. Doubtless there were people who did not support the monarchy, but woe betide anyone trying to leave a cinema before the national anthem marked the end of a the performance.

Of course war had been declared in September 1939 and whilst preparations had been underway for months, not helped by the fascist leanings of much of the aristocracy, a sense of foreboding persisted.

In 1939 London dwarfed all other British cities both in size and influence. Only Glasgow registered a population of over one million whilst London had mushroomed to eight times that size. In every city and town there were the first signs of the impending conflict. Sandbags were piled up outside banks and public buildings. Barrage balloons seemingly placed at random swayed gently in the breeze whilst ancient anti-aircraft guns were placed in Hyde Park.

In spite of the ominous signs many chose to ignore them. The weather remained good and the beaches were packed with holiday crowds enjoying the last of the year's warm sunshine. Many remained confident that the government would come to an agreement with the Germans.

These hopes were finally dashed when on September 1st German troops crossed the Polish border. Most of the Polish air force was destroyed on the ground whilst their horse cavalry was decimated in short order. After an unexplained delay an ultimatum was delivered to Hitler giving him two hours to announce an unconditional withdrawal from all Polish territory.

The foreign secretary Lord Halifax described the last moments of peace in his diary entry for 3rd September: "I went over to Number Ten at eleven o'clock. Great crowds had gathered in Downing Street. At 11.10 still no news. Accordingly the prime minister told the service departments that they might consider themselves to be at war."

Across the country people crowded round their wireless sets to listen to Neville Chamberlain who sounded rather like a favourite uncle delivering bad news as kindly as he could. To hear the gentle but rather tremulous tones of their prime minister hardly inspired confidence. He concluded the broadcast: "Now may God bless you and may he defend the right for it is evil things that we will be fighting, brute force, bad faith, injustice, oppression and persecution, and against them I am certain right will prevail."

The general public were not so sure. Unlike at the outbreak of the Great War there was no flag waving and cheering at the prospect. The euphoria of sunny summer holidays were forgotten as London and other major cities prepared themselves for an immediate onslaught from the air. The Great War had brought a taste of what people expected was yet to come. Spasmodic air raids then had killed 670 people with many more injured. Predictions of massive raids following the declaration of war were terrifying. The eminent scientist J. B. Haldane wrote that he expected the first attack over London would kill between fifty and one hundred thousand citizens. Alarmist? Hardly when compared to the committee of imperial defence whose official estimate was that the opening assault would last two months and six hundred thousand Londoners would die with over one million injured. With the country already on edge within minutes of Chamberlain finishing his address the air raid sirens sounded in London. People dashed to find what cover they could, but luckily it was a false alarm and a prelude to what became known as the phoney war.

Most young children were unaware of the significance of what was unfolding. In East Ham a five year old Jean Picton vividly remembers her grandmother's reaction to the news. Rocking back and forth in her chair she kept repeating "Oh God not again!" The memories of the horrors of the Great War were flooding back. It was as if she could foresee the devastation shortly to be unleashed on the East End.

As the weeks passed the public mood brightened. Perhaps the doomsters were wrong. Rationing and shortages were annoying, but things were still relatively normal. Christmas was celebrated albeit on a reduced scale. On New Year's Eve toasts were made behind blackout curtains. A new decade beckoned. Was it really going to be as dire as many had predicted? As children we had no idea, buoyed by the confidence of youth we looked forward with hope undimmed.

Chapter 3

Home Sweet Home

Was it an omen? The start of 1940 witnessed heavy snowfall across the country. Villages were cut off and in towns and cities rutted roads made getting around really difficult, not helped at night by black-out restrictions.

Constantly feeling cold during the winter months was a common bond remembered by children at that time. No matter whether you lived in a stately pile or a tenement in Glasgow the cold gnawed away at you. Many remembered waking up to see frost had formed inside the window panes.

The great and good were facing a dilemma. Should they sell their London mansions and retreat to their country estates? Some did so only to find their ancient piles requisitioned and then had to hurriedly look for a cottage on the estate or, perish the thought, rent a modest house in the nearest town. Some compromised by moving into one wing only to find the rest of the house taken over by wild evacuees from the East End of London. Possibly even worse was to have the army billeted in the house. All that shouting as troops did some 'square bashing' in front of the historic edifice.

As winter tightened its grip it was a time of chilblains and getting dressed under the bedclothes. Bath nights offered a temporary respite despite only a few inches of water being encouraged by the government. Gerry Southworth was eleven in 1940. A tin bath that normally hung outside their terraced house in Wakefield was brought in. Sitting in the tub in a kitchen warmed by the old fashioned range is a fond memory that remains with him. My mother would make an improvised wigwam out of towels as our bathroom was always perishingly cold. Jean Sporle was four in 1940 and was living in one room with her parents in Hammersmith. They had to cook on the landing and share a toilet with four other families. There was no bathroom and no bath night to look forward to. Just a bowl of water and a quick wash down, teeth chattering as the water cooled so quickly.

The differences between town and country life were accentuated by the war. Whilst there had always been rural poverty, this remained but it was still possible to feed yourself better than your city cousins. Even tied cottages tended to have gardens which were normally turned over to the growing of vegetables. There was also the opportunity to have the occasional rabbit, although poaching was still viewed as the most heinous of crimes by the squirearchy and those caught received stiff sentences.

London was not the only city where extreme wealth and real poverty were near neighbours, sometimes only a street or two separating them. Dust sheets covered many fashionable city homes as their occupants sought the safety of the country, whilst portraits of their ancestors stared down accusingly on the abandoned homes.

During the inter-war years the suburban dream was vigorously championed by builders and developers. Certainly London from its inception had continued to grow and spread, at times in spurts then for a period more sedately, but the creep from the centre continued. This accelerated into a stampede during the 1930s. Vast tracts of what had once been prime agricultural land were gobbled up and sacrificed to bricks, mortar and tarmac. It was as if London was being consumed by some insatiable monster. In 1900 central London was about eight miles from open country. By 1939 the distance had all but doubled. What was it that suburbia offered that was so irresistible?

It was in the late thirties that my parents bought their relatively modest but comfortable house in Edgware for just under a thousand pounds. Edgware was the most north-westerly outpost of the Northern Line tube system. The station built in 1924 served both the West End and the city, both of which could be reached in about forty minutes. Edgware and similar suburbs seemed irresistible. They offered a heady mix of a country lifestyle coupled with easy access to all parts of London. A London transport poster offered country excursions to Edgware. A couple dressed for hiking were captured beside a five-barred gate staring across golden cornfields. The poster was issued in 1926 so by the time my parents arrived Edgware had already grown from a rural village into an urban sprawl dominated by mock Tudor villas. At the time our house was on the extremity of that growth and our garden backed onto open countryside.

So the environment that children grew up in at the outbreak of war was as diverse as it is today. From the grand country homes to the inner city slums was added this hybrid gang of suburban kids. All were going to be affected by the war. For many it would be a life without a father, for others the added horror of bombing. For those living in the country life seemed very little altered. The arrival of evacuees and later American troops left a lasting legacy. Some previous perceptions changed, others endorsed. Later added to the mix of country life were the arrivals of prisoners of war. So it was that although many children did not dwell on the problems confronting their families and the country, they did form the background to their most formative years.

For children even more than adults home should be a place of love and security. Sadly this is not always the case as their family backgrounds are as different as the type of houses they grow up in. There are several books written on the war-time house which suggest a kind of uniformity that is obviously untrue. If there was to be some sort of meeting point it could be possibly found in the suburban home much like my parents'.

Entering through a wooden garden gate there was a lawn on either side of a central path. There was no garage. A small entrance hall had a staircase leading off it to the bedrooms. To the right was a formal sitting room with a substantial three-piece suite and occasional tables. A mirror over a central fireplace and oil paintings in heavy gilt frames. The dining room contained a table with six chairs and comfortable leather studded armchairs either side of the fireplace. Other than the soft furnishings these rooms would not seem totally out of place today. It is in the kitchen where vast differences occur. A long narrow room dominated by a large Welsh dresser and it also had storage cupboards and a rickety old coke boiler. The far end of the kitchen was the work place with a stone sink, a copper and wringer for the Monday wash-day ritual. There was also a north facing larder. There were none of today's gadgets and cooking was done on a temperamental gas cooker. Upstairs the bedrooms, apart from mine, were large and all eiderdowns and candlewick bedspreads. The bathroom, like the kitchen, would be considered archaic. A white enamelled bath, a pedestal wash-basin and an airing cupboard (a minor source of heat) offset by the freezing linoleum floor.

All of this offered comparative luxury when compared to the home of Albert Knight who lived in what is now gentrified Islington. Back in the 1940s the houses where bankers, fund managers and celebrities live today steered on just the right side of slum dwellings, albeit most of the houses were Georgian or Victorian. Then they were often split into several homes within the one house. Albert lived in Darne Street and he reckoned the house was fairly typical of many throughout the capital. The kitchen was in the basement and contained a solid fuel brick copper. The dining room had a wrought-iron range which had to be cleaned daily with blacking. There was a tiny living room and three small bedrooms on the ground floor. There was a toilet but no bathroom. Linoleum rather than carpets lined the floors and lighting was supplied by wall mounted gas lights. With no regular deliveries of coal his mother was sometimes unable to cook. When the coal-man did eventually call he arrived on a horse drawn cart. The coal-man wore a sort of leather hood that covered his head and shoulders. He heaved the sacks through a grill into a coal shed in their pocket-sized back garden.

Even that very basic standard of living compared well to many country cottages. It seems extraordinary to us today that so recently in our history very many dwellings remained without electricity. Some cottages in Theddingworth in Leicestershire also continued to exist without running water, which had to be drawn daily from a well in the back yard. Here furnishings remained unaltered from Victorian times. The kitchen did not even contain a sink and clothes had to be washed by slapping the soapy garments against a huge stone in the yard. Meals were taken at a scrubbed pine table and the damp on the walls was partially covered by old samplers. Upstairs in the stark, bare, cold bedrooms large families often arranged for their children to sleep head to toe. And yet within a few miles there were several large mansions. For the time being the wealthy eked out the last of their pre-war luxuries before they too had to endure being moved or forced to live cheek by jowl with strangers.

Cold, darkness and Celtic melancholy are the earliest abiding memories of Arthur Price-Jones who lived on the Welsh borders with his parents and brother. His father was a miller by trade, which was a reserved occupation and accordingly was not required to enlist. Despite this he saw little of his dad who often worked a seven day week and spent much of his spare time working on his allotment. Perhaps this led to Arthur never having a close bond with him whilst to the young boy his mother always appeared exhausted. The sheer grind of war-time Britain was pervasive, Arthur remembers, and that sense remained with him.

A rare moment of excitement in this grey world even had the neighbours appearing from behind their curtains and standing on the street as a lorry from the flour mill pulled up. They watched as the carcass of a pig was off-loaded. Arthur's father belonged to a 'pig club' and this delivery was the result of his dad's long investment in the club over many months. The pig was proudly suspended on meat hooks in an outside disused lavatory. Once again the anticipation was better than the reality. The meat was tough and the bacon very fatty.

This feeling of raised hopes not realised was confirmed by memories of Christmas. Like many his pillow-slip contained an exotic orange and a box of sweet and sickly dates. What Arthur longed for was a bike. What he got was a wooden scooter that his father had made. No doubt a great deal of work had gone into the making, but children can be very self-centred and ungrateful. Other years Arthur remembers getting rather dull books or clockwork toys that did not work properly. It was not until Arthur started his primary education that he began to realise that life had much more to offer than what he had experienced so far. It prompted a desire for learning which led ultimately to a very successful and happy life.

Before he could reach for the sky he had to overcome a truly frightening illness. Scarlet Fever was one of the most feared children's diseases. During the nineteenth century it killed around twenty percent of those infected. The symptoms included a cough, sore throat and an ugly red rash. The tongue often became lumpy and swollen. Arthur and his brother were rushed to hospital and placed in isolation. The hospital had formerly served as a Victorian workhouse and not much had changed for it was still a grim and forbidding place. Being so ill only snatches are remembered, but the smell of antiseptic and the gruel-like food linger still. Restored to their home they were given large clockwork racing cars. Still no bike!

It is perhaps a reflection on Arthur's childhood that one of the few highlights was attending Sunday school, something that many children resented having been forced to attend by their parents. Religion was central to life in the Welsh borders, with many active non-conformist chapels. Sunday afternoon was given over to religious instruction for the local children. Luckily for Arthur, Miss Freeman the teacher read them stories from magazines rather than from the bible. Arthur guessed that theology was not her strong point, but he remembers her as being warm, kind and friendly, a beacon in his rather grey world.

Of all the innovations in housing during the twenties and thirties, by far the most important was the installation of electricity. By the outbreak of war roughly seventy percent of houses had been connected. The roll-out had been hampered by having so many companies involved rather than a central supplier. The effect of electricity on family life was profound, not least amongst children. For centuries youngsters had been obsessed with stories of ghosts and spooky figures appearing. These were often prompted by poor lighting which continued with the use of gas lamps. Children's imaginations ran wild and although even youngsters today can be drawn into believing, it is normally because they want to experience for a few moments the alarm genuinely felt by youngsters over previous centuries.

There had been a proliferation of new electric household gadgets during the 1930s that was brought to a halt as production was switched to the war effort. Women welcomed the arrival of hairdryers and curlers and even electric floor polishers. The spin-off for electrical goods seemed endless as electric irons and kettles were welcomed into the nation's homes. Housework was further reduced as vacuum cleaners confined manual carpet sweepers to history. These additions did not come without risks and many products were unreliable. Reports started coming in of careless users giving themselves electric shocks and some deaths were even recorded.

Electricity also created real job opportunities as electricians were in constant demand, although apprenticeships were curtailed at the outbreak of war due to the military now undertaking much of the training. For children the use of clockwork toys was extended by the war. For most an electric train set remained a distant dream.

Of more pressing concern for most families was safety from the bombing that was still expected in the near future. Dining tables were sold or stored away as Morrison shelters were made available by the end of 1940. It is unique in being the only article of quasi furniture whose life span only covered five years. Named after the Minister for Home Defence Herbert Morrison, it was installed in thousands of houses. The height of a normal dining table, it measured roughly six feet by four feet. It doubled up as a dining table for the family but underneath a mattress could be laid for sleeping. Its sides were covered in wire mesh designed to help with flying debris. The shelter saved many lives giving protection from falling bricks and masonry. Many children spent nights sleeping as German aircraft droned above only to be wakened by frightening flashes and explosions. For five years this ugly but functional addition to family life was centre stage for meals and even celebrations at Christmas. It was delivered free for those earning less than £350 a year. For those earning more a charge of £7 was made which was not a lot if it was to save lives. The snag was that the householders had to assemble the shelter themselves (shades of Ikea to come). With so many men away from home lots of youngsters were able to show off their practical skills.

Another politician Sir John Anderson gave his name to the other domestic shelter made available by the government. This was suitable for those whose living space was restricted but who were fortunate enough to have a garden. The Anderson had the advantage of being simple to manufacture, cheap to supply and easy to erect. It consisted of two curved sections of corrugated steel which were bolted together at the top. It then needed to be sunk some three feet into the ground with the entrance being protected by a steel shield. It was then necessary to spread the soil that had been dug out over the structure to give added protection. The shelter, although crude, proved remarkably effective. Without a direct hit it was likely all sheltering would survive. Maybe, but stories of cold wet nights spent in Anderson shelters are still vividly remembered. After a while some chose warmth rather than safety, occasionally with tragic results.

So home life for children was hard. Indeed harsh in comparison to today's children. Yet it is strange how many of those living then look back at their wartime experiences with pleasure. Is it just that nostalgic memories clouded over time? A settled upbringing is reckoned to be important for a child's development, yet for most youngsters life was anything but settled. Absent fathers, sometimes being wrenched from their homes. Still the bombs fell, still food was scarce and pleasures were simple. For those living in towns and cities those very bombs provided an exciting playground. Youngsters were allowed to roam freely with relatively little traffic to interrupt games of football and cricket. There must have been those traumatised by events but it was rarely in evidence. For most small treats were anticipated with huge excitement. The buying of a comic with your pocket money or the promise of a second-hand toy for a birthday present. Anticipation rather than reality is what spurs children on, and thoughts of the next meal no matter how basic were never far away.

Chapter 4

'Vaccies'

Children are normally the innocent bystanders in war but by September 1939 they were elevated to take central stage. The evacuation of children from the major industrial cities was a monumental exercise carried out with minute planning and military precision.

Astonishingly plans were already being drawn up as early as 1924 and confirmed the following year with the setting up of a committee to consider the effects of air attacks on the civilian population of London. This had been prompted by the spasmodic air attacks during the Great War. Although only several hundred people had been killed, the advance of technology and a continuing mistrust of Germany supported their prudence. With genuine concerns that raids would start within days of war being declared and the effect on civilian morale, the detailed plans were set in motion.

In July 1939 the government released a series of leaflets on civil defence which were delivered to every home in Great Britain. One was devoted to evacuation headed 'Why and How'. This set out in detail how the plan was going to be implemented. The areas designated caused some disagreement as some were quite near city centres that were deemed neutral zones. Those areas that were to be evacuated included large swathes of London together with the Medway towns. Other places in danger of early attack included ports like Portsmouth, Southampton, Hull, Liverpool and Glasgow. Places with high density populations like Birmingham, Sheffield, Newcastle and Edinburgh were also included.

The authorities had already established the amount of accommodation available in towns and rural areas unlikely to be attacked from the air, together with reception posts that would receive and deploy the evacuees. In preparation all teachers were required to attend their schools on 26th August, despite the schools still being on holiday. They were briefed and informed that they may only receive a few hours notice to start the evacuation. The following week children were called back to school to take part in a full evacuation rehearsal. Each child was required to carry their gas mask and a case with clothes and food for the journey. Each school was identified by a number given to them and advised of their departure point. For the children all this was new and exciting and those worried were reassured that this was only a practice and it was unlikely that they would really have to leave their homes.

As the news grew worse it was decided that evacuation would actually start on 1st September. Posters started appearing in schools giving times for mothers with children below school age to assemble. They were required to write the name of the child on a label that would be tied or sewn onto the kid's clothing. Older children were allowed to take one toy in addition to their clothes and food. The whole exercise must have seemed surreal and yet all but a tiny minority conformed.

Within hours of the government order thousands of women who were to act as escorts and support the teachers were contacted, and so started the greatest mass evacuation of children ever attempted. 'An exodus bigger than that of Moses' was how Walter Elliot the Minister of Health described it. Waves of children descended on train and bus stations. Newsreels showed parents waving goodbye to their children as giant locomotives wheezed and spluttered as they took their excited passengers off into the unknown. In reality most parents were denied access to platforms as it was reckoned that a swift and unemotional departure was best for all concerned.

For many children it was like the beginning of a holiday and a great adventure. Undoubtedly there was comfort in being surrounded by brothers or sisters and familiar teachers. What they saw outside the windows was certainly not familiar. Many from the slums and tenements had never even seen fields before. Definitely not cattle and sheep and all those miles of open space. For some that initial excitement was already cooling. Life was going to be really different. Where had all the people gone? The crowded streets, the factories, the smoke?

The next shock for the children came when they were off-loaded onto a bleak platform in a strange town. From there they were normally transported by bus to a civic or village hall to be processed. For many this was an extremely painful process. Adults wandered in and picked their chosen child, seemingly at random. There were floods of tears as brothers and sisters were separated. Many spoke of the girls being picked first as they were reckoned to be less trouble. Those left to the very end were made to feel doubly unwanted.

Being taken by strangers to an unfamiliar house or cottage must have been frightening. Obviously the welcome these kids from our inner cities had varied enormously, but the overall impression appears to have been one of mutual suspicion. The householder had to accept the children if they had a spare room. Some grew to love their adopted parents and kept in touch throughout their lives, but others could not wait to get home despite the bombs.

There were stories of dirty lice-ridden children being foisted on resentful home owners, but in truth most of the children were well scrubbed and wearing their best clothes. There were of course horror stories. A young lad billeted in Batley had his new leather shoes swapped for wooden clogs and others reported being fed just bread and jam, with disgusting tripe being served as the main meal of the day. A wonderful film 'Escaping the Blitz' also records children being housed in a stately home. They were crowded into dormitories in the west wing. The rest of the house was given over to friendly Land Army girls, whilst the lady of the manor grumbled away in the east wing resenting both the children and the cheeky Land Army girls. Life had truly been turned upside down. Perhaps the worst example of misunderstanding related to Jewish children who were forced to eat pork. The farmers they had been staying with did not understand why the youngsters were turning down perfectly good food that others would have thought to be a treat.

For many children the open countryside offered a freedom to wander and explore. Some were taught old country skills and were asked to help work on farms. The most animosity appeared to come from other children and many loathed going to school where endless fights and skirmishes tended to break out in the playground. Another cause of tension stemmed rather surprisingly from city kids being ahead of their country cousins in their schoolwork. The impression, particularly in village schools, was the lack of ambition shown for the pupils by their teachers. Most of the students were children of agricultural workers whose horizons were rarely raised by the teachers beyond the endless repetition of their times tables. Many were still taught using chalk and slates. The one norm in all the schools was strict discipline. A whack with a ruler was not unusual and at public schools the cane was still administered regularly.

During the first phase of evacuation some children were sent away with their mothers. My sister and I were packed off with my mother to deepest Devon. It was only a matter of weeks before we returned home to take our chances.

Jean Sporle was evacuated with her mother to a village just outside Manchester called Roe Green near Worsley. They stayed for two years and were made really welcome by the family they were billeted with that included two young sons, who Jean soon came to think of as her brothers. Unlike many, Jean's experience was of a warm welcome from everyone. She soon acquired a Manchester accent which took her some time to lose when she returned to London.

The most vivid account of a youngster being evacuated comes from Ronnie Pitt who was born in 1939. He lived with his parents in Kensington. Not the posh part with its luxury shops and smart Georgian houses. They lived on the ground floor of a four-bedroomed house in North Kensington. By 1942 the Luftwaffe was extending its bombing of London westwards and Ronnie's parents decided it was time for their two sons to be evacuated. Ronnie remembers being taken to Kings Cross station by his mother. There was a tearful farewell as the young lad was handed over to a lady wearing a red arm-band. It was the first time he had been separated from his mother and brother. His father had already left home to serve abroad and now all remaining links with a happy home life suddenly appeared broken. He was sad and bemused rather than frightened. Carrying his gas-mask and with a cardboard label tied round his neck, he was given a box containing food. It was explained to him that it was for his lunch and he was not to eat it for a couple of hours. Food can be a great comforter. It was all gone before the train left the platform.

The journey seemed to last forever. It was too hot in the compartment, but once the window was opened they were covered in soot particles. He was initially seated with weeping children. A lady tried to comfort them and eventually they all fell asleep. At last the train shuddered to a halt and along with about thirty other children he staggered out onto the platform. He had arrived in a small town called Market Harborough. They were all led onto a green single-decker bus. This was the first of many shocks. Surely buses were supposed to be red and double-deckers!

With a grinding of gears they set off into the unknown. There were a series of stops and names were called out and one by one his companions departed. Eventually it was Ronnie's turn.

Memories of getting to his new home were vague but he did learn many years later that he had been far from welcome. The lady he came to know as Aunty Grace had to accept an evacuee because she had a spare bedroom and she had hoped to be allocated a girl. He remembers there was another lady in the house who became his Aunty May. There was also a daughter called Grace (his first boy-hood crush) and a daughter called Isabel who was away at the time serving in the forces. Aunty Grace was married to Joe who was a gardener at a large local estate.

He was shown up to his small bedroom. He was told that the village that was to be his home was called Sibbertoft. It was in the county of Northamptonshire and slap bang in the middle of England about as far away from the sea as it was possible. The house had no toilet or bathroom. Washing was done at an old sink and baths taken once a week were in a tin bath that hung on a wall in a passage between the two small cottages. There was an outside toilet at the end of the garden. Flushing was done with a bucket of water drawn from an ancient pump. All very basic but at least he did not have to share a bed for the first time in his life.

Life for many evacuees was something of a culture shock. They found the lack of traffic and street noise eerie, to be replaced by the sound of sheep grazing or more frighteningly the squeals of cattle being slaughtered. From the hectic life of central London Ronnie was confronted with a village with just a few streets logically called Front Street, Back Street and Middle Street. The village also sported a pub, a single shop, a parish church dating back to the 13th century and a chapel.

Here was another change in Ronnie's life. Aunty Grace was religious and each Sunday her extended family trooped off to chapel. At the time the divide between denominations was very noticeable. In the neighbouring town of Market Harborough chapel folk tended to shop at outlets run by one of their own, as did those attending the parish church. Roman Catholics were still viewed with suspicion, whilst contact with Jews was confined to those touring the countryside selling cloth and items of haberdashery. The visit of one good-looking hawker ensured he enjoyed a regular trade as his visits were eagerly anticipated particularly by the younger women.

It seems strange to us that only eighty years ago life was very different with so many still relying on water from wells and others on gas lamps for their lighting. Despite this Ronnie settled in very happily. There was only one other evacuee at the village school and unlike many in his situation he found no animosity towards him from the other children. Trouble tended to break out where evacuee kids outnumbered the locals.

Although there was strict rationing, food was more plentiful in the countryside. Vegetables and fruit were always available. Berries were gathered from the hedgerows and bottled in Kilner jars to be enjoyed during the bleak winter months. Apples were wrapped in newspaper to preserve them, and runner beans and potatoes were grown in the garden. Ronnie was fed three meals a day and their rations were sometimes supplemented by a brace of pheasants. No questions asked and none given on how they were acquired.

After Sunday lunch the family went for a walk while at other times their pleasures were simple. Reading, listening to the wireless and board games helped fill leisure time. There was a local airfield and the children used to watch the Wellington bombers flying low over their heads. The airmen used to congregate at the local pub which was very much out of bounds as Aunty Grace warned the youngsters of the dangers of the demon drink. Not a view shared by Ronnie's father who on occasional visits to Sibbertoft would set off in the opposite direction to the pub before doubling back and enjoying a couple of pints.

Despite being happy living with his adopted family throughout the war, the strangeness of country life continued to be vivid in Ronnie's memory. A funeral where the coffin was drawn to the church on a farm wagon by an old carthorse, with the streets lined with neighbours dressed in black. In 1945 Ronnie returned to London but his contact with the family and the village has now extended to over seventy years.

Evacuation is viewed from an opposite perspective by Martin van Oppen in East Langton, a Leicestershire village about ten miles distant from Sibbertoft. Here was no warm and comforting welcome for a raft of tough kids from the East End of London. Today we may have described their behaviour as challenging, that some were out of control and considered by locals to be a bloody nuisance. Forget the war raging across Europe and the far east, this was village war conducted with similar passion.

With the outbreak of war and with a name like van Oppen life was never going to be easy for a young lad. The family was well to do and had lived in England for generations and were of Dutch extraction. No matter, even before the arrival of the evacuees Martin and his two brothers were labelled as Krauts or Boche. Children can be very cruel but it led to the brothers being able to handle themselves as a result of constant jibes and taunts. The arrival of the 'vaccies' as they were known saw the van Oppen boys welcomed into the village army intent on facing down the invaders. This was a situation more commonly played out than is generally acknowledged. It is doubtful in this case who was most to blame. Certainly even the adult villagers made it clear the Londoners were not welcome. It was as if they came from another planet. Local youngsters were brought up to respect authority, be it teachers or the leading local landowner. Not this group, they literally thumbed their noses at attempts to control them. They missed the smoke, the bustle and camaraderie of their fellow East Enders. These country cousins were a load of stuck-up snooty snobs.

Many of the incomers went out of their way to antagonise, releasing chickens from their pens and stampeding cattle. It seemed that the two sets of youngsters had nothing in common other than the desire to fight each other.

Martin's grandmother was an imposing matriarch. She lived in The Grange, the largest, most imposing house in the village. She was regularly seen driving full tilt around the surrounding countryside in her large Vauxhall, blaring on the horn particularly at the evacuees who knew to run for cover when they heard her coming. Martin and his brothers also lived in a substantial house with their mother. The social divide was always more noticeable in the country where in the village most still had to draw their water from a pump on the village green. 'The rich man in his castle, the poor man at his gate' seemingly still accepted by most.

Martin remembers an incident that underlines the mutual mistrust often felt by groups from different social backgrounds. Martin's mother employed a young nursery maid from Coventry. For a couple of weeks everything went well until the arrival of an unexpected visitor. This came in the shape of a newly born baby, the result of the nursery maid's affair with an American soldier. The girl was sacked and asked to leave. She did, taking Martin's mother's bicycle and a canteen of silver cutlery belonging to the family. The baby in a basket strapped to the handlebars, with the canteen in a pannier on the back. The police were called and the girl arrested within the hour. Today confronted with a similar problem the situation would have probably been dealt with more sympathetically .As such presumably nothing would then have been stolen. But it is wrong to impose modern thinking on a situation that happened some eighty years ago. It was a harsher world and one assumes that both parties could have justified their behaviour.

As the phoney war continued, and even with the start of the Blitz, many from the inner cities chose to bring their children home. But as the dangers to civilian life rose and fell only to rise again, a second and third wave of evacuations took place as V1 and V2 buzz-bombs fell towards the end of the war. Hitler was playing his last terrifying card.

However evacuation had proved to be a outstanding logistical success, but it also highlighted many of the problems to plague Britain in the post war years. For some like Ronnie it opened up the possibility of a different type of life, but for many it underlined the changes in society which were long overdue.

Chapter 5

Bunking Off

No matter whether a youngster attended Eton or an inner city or village school, they were all subject to strict discipline. The old adage 'Spare the rod, spoil the child' lingered on. Children were subjected to raps on the knuckle with a ruler, chalk hurled at them and clips round the ear for minor transgressions. The cane was used for more serious misbehaviour. It was a matter of pride not to cry out in pain, to never give the teacher that satisfaction, by biting your lip and taking what was coming in mute defiance. It was usually no use complaining to your parents as they normally supported the teacher's action. At my prep school I was hauled up to a dais where the chemistry master perched, for the sin of talking in class. Told to stick out my tongue the teacher used a pair of tongs to apply some powder which he extracted from a test tube. My tongue was still sore by the time I returned home. Rather than be horrified or outraged by this little pocket dictator, my mother simply said it should encourage me not to talk in class again. Different times, different perceptions.

With so many young teachers serving in the forces it was largely left to women and older men to educate the young. This in no way led to a fall in discipline. The class stood up whenever a teacher entered the room. At grammar and public school older masters swept through the corridors in their flowing gowns. Pupils were seated at lidded wooden desks where they could store their books and possessions. These desks were often covered in ancient graffiti or long forgotten names gouged into the surface by a penknife.

At elementary schools girls were taught domestic science and needlework, whilst boys had lessons in metal and woodwork. It was as if the youngsters' futures were being guided by the authorities, their horizons regulated. In rural areas many village schools had only one classroom to accommodate all ages. Often the older children were asked to help out with the teaching of the youngest. Once again this had the effect of lowering ambition. It was assumed that agricultural workers' children would follow their fathers employed on the local estate. In these backwaters clever children were viewed with as much suspicion as a clever and intelligent woman. Everyone was still expected to know their place, but those old perceptions were already under attack. Those trying to maintain the social order were fighting a losing battle.

School uniform was introduced in many places in an attempt to protect those who could not afford smart clothes. However, uniforms were not cheap but generally a certain uniformity was achieved. With clothes rationed dressing children was a constant struggle. For young boys the standard dress was grey short trousers, a shirt and a pullover in the school colours. A sturdy overcoat and scarf were also essential, with many opting for balaclavas during the coldest weather. For girls many were confined to gymslips together with a shirt and tie. Their short white 'bobby socks' in sharp contrast to their brothers' wrinkled socks, which often fell down to their ankles as the elastic gave way.

Games were also segregated at elementary schools. If there was a play area the girls tended to be confined to netball, whilst at private schools hockey and lacrosse were usually also played. Many state schools did not have playing fields so football and cricket had to be played on tarmac. In contrast public schools usually had wonderful sports facilities, some even had their own swimming pools. Cricket was played in front of thatched pavilions, whilst alongside there were acres of rugby and football pitches. The disparity was and remains astounding, and yet as ever champions emerged from the most unlikely backgrounds. Those attending private schools were hardly pampered. If they boarded they lived in monastic hardship. This was a harsh environment meant to spawn the next generation to serve the soon to be reduced empire. Cross country runs, cold showers and dreadful food was the order of the day. Boxing was also considered to be important in toughening up the next generation. As well as official inter-school tournaments, some schools introduced what was known as a 'round robin'. The class or group were formed into two circles. One set would jog round in a clockwise direction, the other anti-clockwise. All wore boxing gloves. When the master blew his whistle those facing each other had to fight for one minute. Sometimes the pupils were evenly matched, other times you might find the biggest lad fighting the smallest. This tended to result in a group of very tough smaller boys.

The master only stepped in if he thought serious damage was being done. Bloody noses was no excuse to halt the fight. Many of these deprivations inflicted on the young appear barbaric today and yet they seemingly did not do any lasting harm. There was an expectation that boys should develop into tough resourceful men, whilst it was expected that girls should become home-makers and mothers. Everyone in their ordained place, but the effects of the war was going to change all that.

Anyone who was unlucky enough to have eaten 'school dinners' during the war will never forget the smell of over-cooked cabbage that lingers yet. No food eaten since ever tasted or smelt so disgusting. Perhaps part of the problem stemmed from the fact that few schools had their own kitchen. The food pre-cooked, arrived in metal containers and as the lids were lifted so the ghastly smell wafted its way down corridors giving pupils prior warning of the treat to come. There were slithers of meat whose origin was impossible to define. Surely not lamb or beef. Horse perhaps? The offering was covered in a thick gelatinous gravy.

Fish at least smelt different but was no more appetising. Possibly snoek or other fish normally only given to cats. The watery cabbage or sprouts added to the horrible overall effect. Sometimes puddings did offer some respite. Jam roly-poly and lumpy custard sank quickly to the pit of young stomachs lying heavily, until they got home for a tea often consisting of just bread and jam. Because food was so severely rationed it took this generation of kids some years to appreciate that food could offer real pleasure and enjoyment. It was not for nothing that Britain had the reputation for having the worst cuisine in Europe.

School, particularly in the inner cities, was frequently interrupted by air raid warnings. 'Moaning Minnie' as the warning siren was known remains a vivid memory. On first hearing the warning all the pupils were herded into a cellar or a place giving some protection. The drill was practised continually and was usually carried out with the minimum of fuss. During raids some lessons were continued, but it was often a chance for the children to have a sing-song to raise their spirits.

The East End of London, particularly East Ham where Jean Picton lived, was one of the most heavily bombed. All those attending her school lived within a few streets of the Victorian building. She remembers one particularly bizarre event from that time. Her class was instructed by their teacher that on the word 'go' they were to run as fast as they could to their respective houses. On arrival they were instructed to go into their back garden, touch their Anderson shelter and tear back again to school. Sticking to the script Jean rushed past her startled mother into the garden touching the shelter as instructed. "Can't stop" she shouted, red faced and already out of breath. Running back through the house her mother asked her, "What on earth is going on?" Intent on getting back before any of her friends Jean had no time to answer. Her teacher was waiting back at the school, stop-watch in hand checking in even the stragglers. Jean has no idea what her teacher was aiming to achieve other than trying to divert the kids' attention from the previous night's raid that had left much of the surrounding neighbourhood still smoking and flattened.

At the beginning of 1943 Luftwaffe tactics changed with a series of daylight raids undertaken by light bombers. Civilians were strafed in the streets and trains and trolley-buses were machine gunned. More ominously two schools were targeted and seriously damaged. Fortunately these raids took place at daybreak before the students arrived, but worse was to come.

Defences in South East London were minimal with not even barrage balloons being employed. A Focke-Wulf fighter bomber swooped on Coopers Lane school in Woolwich letting loose a volley of machine gun fire. Miraculously no-one was killed but the Luftwaffe pilots were not done yet. The next target was Sandhurst Road school in Catford. A one hundred and ten pound bomb was dropped. It penetrated the side of the building smashing through to the ground floor. It was about a minute before it exploded, giving some children just enough time to escape through broken windows. Those students eating their lunch in the next door dining room were caught in the horrific blast that followed. Thirty eight children along with some of their teachers were killed, with many more seriously injured. Photographs show the bodies covered in sheets lying in the playground.

The authorities did their best to suppress the news, but astonishingly the Germans boasted of the success of the attack in a broadcast made from occupied Paris. There was outrage and not only targeted at the barbaric Germans. Questions were asked as to why were no alarms raised? For a time schools continued to be targeted. It appeared that the war had entered a new low as newspapers condemned the 'fiendish onslaught of a barbarous foe' and mothers understandably started keeping their children at home and truancy rates soared.

It was against this frightening background that my formal education started. My very first day at school was marked by tears and controversy. Edgware elementary school was a good half hour's walk from our house. It took even longer that morning as my mother had to drag me as I protested that I did not want to go. Why did I have to go? I would promise to go next week if she just allowed me to miss the next few days. My pleas fell on stony ground as I was guided into the reception class and left with a sea of new faces and the scary Miss Arnold. Firstly we all had to answer the register. Simply replying 'here' was not acceptable. 'Present, Miss Arnold' was the only response that this seemingly fierce lady would acknowledge. School in my mind was not shaping up well. It was worse than I had imagined. There was a small yard which served as a playground for the infants, before they encountered the rest of the school's pupils. Whilst milk was being distributed during our first break, I slipped out of a side gate that led to an alley that I knew brought me out onto the High Street. I received a few quizzical stares as this small figure made his way home. Except it was not my house that I was seeking. I knew exactly the route that Jack's milk round took and it was not long before I was sitting alongside the milkman as the horse drawn cart continued on its round. He did question why I was not at school, but I lied and told him it did not start until the following week. Meantime, my mother had been rung by the school to say that I had gone missing. Had I been snatched or kidnapped? It may have passed through my mother's mind, but she was confident where she would find me and she was right. With a clip round the ear, I was dragged off screaming. This time my father did give me a lecture that night and I was threatened with all sorts of punishments if I repeated my disappearing act.

Next morning, still protesting, I was again dragged off to school. This time the ticking off came from Miss Arnold and I was required for a time to stand in the corner with my face to the wall. Just to compound my bad behaviour, I refused to take my place in the class when asked to do so. I pretended I had not heard and remained facing the wall. Miss Arnold was furious, but the laughter from my fellow pupils spurred me on. The ability to make people laugh continued to haunt my progress through my schooldays, although sometimes even teachers found it difficult not to join in if the mood took them. I had survived the second day and my parents must have thought that I had finally settled in. Unfortunately I had not. Once again I made my escape at the first break. This time my mother cut me off before I could locate the milkman. Retribution was swift. I was carted back to school and the furious Miss Arnold. 'Did I want to be a delinquent?' she asked. I had no idea what that meant. I thought everyone was being unreasonable. A second scolding from my father, coupled with the threat of the cane, ensured that my truancy days were over. One positive that came out of my behaviour was that Ann Dempsey, the prettiest girl in the class, thought I was really brave and rewarded me for a time with kisses as we chased round the playground. Perhaps school was not so bad after all. Even Miss Arnold was being kind as I grappled with learning to read and write. Ann's liking for me was short lived as she told me I had sticky-out ears. I knew I had sticky-out ears, anyway my friends from now on would be boys. Girls were too fickle.

Propaganda had a strange effect on children's minds. I imagined Germans to be almost sub-human, looking like monsters from a horror film. It, therefore, came as a complete shock when in 1944 a group of German prisoners of war were detailed to repair a wall at our school, which had been damaged by a bomb that had fallen nearby. They were guarded by a couple of soldiers whose attitude did not seem to suggest that the young Germans posed any threat. Although we were told not to go near them in our break, our curiosity got the better of us. They were not monsters, they were friendly, beckoning us towards them or calling out hello. One was blond and very good looking. Trust Ann Dempsey to be the first to go over to them. Gradually we all followed carefully, as if approaching a caged tiger. The guards told us to scram, but they did not seem too concerned. One POW spoke a little English and we replied to his questions before a teacher ordered us away. It was all so confusing. These young men were not wild beasts, they were friendly and strangely attractive, but as Miss Arnold reminded us, not long ago they had been trying to kill us. I would have to ask my sister what she thought. She was always wise about such matters.

As the war dragged on, school life changed very little. We still had air raid warnings but they became less frequent. Shrapnel was harder to come by and its currency in the school swap market less important. Now cigarette cards were supreme. They were all issued before the war and were much prized, particularly those featuring sports stars such as footballers and cricketers. Collections were made and lost playing flickers, a game that could be played wherever there was a wall and involved attempting to flick your card to cover your opponents, thus adding to your collection. In the autumn conkers took precedence. Prize specimens were baked in ovens or soaked in brine in an attempt to toughen the outer skins. More often than not the conker was defeated from within, as the string cut into the softer inner and the prize weapon became lopsided and ultimately useless.

Life assumed a routine and my behaviour improved when I left Miss Arnold's class for the next year. Apart from the head all the other teachers were ladies, with so many men serving in the forces. Each morning I made the long trek to school whatever the weather, often arriving soaked to the skin. The smell of wet young bodies in the cloakroom is another smell that remains with me. Pocket money was just a few coppers and had to be spent wisely. A favourite purchase was a bag of Smith's crisps with the magic twist of blue paper that contained the salt. We also bought ice cream of sorts from the milk bar in the High Street. It was run by an ex-professional wrestler who was built like a wardrobe. I have never seen anyone of his stature since. He always wore a white coat that fought to contain his girth. There were no wafers in those days and his take on ice cream was served in a paper container, the type used today for cup cakes. Ever optimistic I always hoped that it would taste like the ice cream that was available before the war that had been described to me. It did not. It was foul and tasted of potato. None of us ever had the courage to tell the giant as he towered over us. As soon as we were out of sight we threw the gooey mess at the nearest wall and watched it stick like glue. The nearest I ever got to eating a delicious ice cream at that time was in Selfridges. Even then as I tucked into the strawberry ice cream served in a smart metal bowl, an air raid warning had my mother escorting me to the basement and the opportunity lost.

Learning at the school was not too demanding on the teachers. Their mission appeared to be confined to us all learning to read and write and to be able to add, subtract, multiply and divide. The pace of learning was regulated by the progress of the slowest in the class and so became rather boring. Most learning was done by repetition as we endlessly parroted 'one times twelve is twelve, two times twelves are twenty four' right through the entire table until it was ingrained in our minds forever. Sums were the most difficult because everything had to be calculated in pounds, shillings and pence. The only other lessons tended to be tub-thumping history lessons, telling us how proud we should be of Britain and its Empire. And we were proud, proud that we had stood alone against Germany until the Yanks joined us. With the end of the war we celebrated with street parties and parties at school. How we cheered when the first British jet plane streaked over our school to much excitement.

Leaving the security of home to start school is usually difficult for both mother and child made more so due to a background of war and falling bombs. All were affected no matter how privileged. From the cloisters of public schools to those of villages and inner cities, the 1940s were our formative years. A unique time but one that most continue to look back on as being generally happy, a time that served us well for the challenges ahead.

Chapter 6

All Hell Let Loose

As the harsh winter of 1940 gave way to spring most children had only the vaguest idea of how the war was developing. Those old enough to understand knew that somehow the retreat and evacuation of troops from Dunkirk was rated as a victory, while the threat to Britain was tightening with the fall of France and the occupation of the Channel Islands just a few miles distant from our shores.

Hitler had been planning the invasion of Britain under the code-name Sea Lion. His ardour had been cooled somewhat by significant losses to his navy and it was Goering who persuaded him that the might of the Luftwaffe could crush the Royal Air Force and allow access to the mainland. This was a significant misjudgement as British airmen were joined by French and Polish pilots who had found their way to England. The Poles particularly gained a reputation for almost insane bravery.

So it was over the glorious summer months that the Battle of Britain was fought and won. Those living in the south of England became used to seeing dog-fights taking place above them. Not only in the skies over the Channel and ports, but also the open fields of Sussex and Surrey, extending at times to suburban London. My mother told me she remembered holding me in her arms in our garden as planes chased each other across the sky. It was like watching some deadly ballet. In neighbouring gardens shouts of encouragement and raised fists urged our boys on oblivious to the danger to themselves.

The Germans designated 13th August 'The Day of the Eagle' which triggered the start of the Battle of Britain. All through August the Luftwaffe strove to gain ascendancy by bombing coastal towns and taking out RAF stations in the south. To do this they were sustaining huge losses of aircraft as resistance was far stronger than anticipated. On 15th September they ordered an all-out assault. This day became known as Battle of Britain Day. It proved catastrophic for the Germans with the Luftwaffe sustaining record losses. After a lull the following day attacks were resumed on 17th September while the following day was again quiet over the southern skies. It was obvious to both sides that the Luftwaffe had failed to achieve ascendancy of the skies needed for a land invasion. Operation Sea Lion was cancelled and Hitler had suffered his first major setback of the war. Luftwaffe General Werner Kreipe later stated that the decision to try and destroy the RAF had marked a turning point in the outcome of the world war. Whilst the victory of ¦the few' was wonderful for the morale of the country, there was to be no respite particularly for the population of London.

It was a glorious summer's day and young Terry Norton was walking in a field just outside Wallingford in Surrey. He paused thinking he could hear a strange humming noise, but then assuming that he was mistaken he continued on his way but the drone increased. Suddenly there was no sunlight and glancing skyward he was alarmed to see a swarm of German fighters and bombers flying in tight formation. He had become used to seeing skirmishes above as RAF and Luftwaffe planes grappled for ascendancy, but this was different, frightening and ominous as the massive formation headed towards London.

At the end of August the German news bureau announced that current raids were only a prelude. 'The decisive blow was about to fall.' For once the German propaganda machine was not lying. That lovely summer's day, 7th September was the beginning of the nightmare that would become known as 'The Blitz'. For eight months and five days London was hammered. At its height there were fifty seven days of consecutive bombing. By the time Terry got home to tell his mother, the first bombs were already raining down. It was five o'clock by the time the planes reached their target. An hour later the aircraft had all departed leaving behind a scene of chaos and panic.

There was hardly time to deal with the dead and injured before the raiders returned at eight o'clock. The River Thames, the very source of London's growth and prosperity, now acted as a magnet for its intended destruction lit as it was by bright moonlight. Timber warehouses lining the docks were set ablaze. A paint factory was hit and a barge containing sugar was set alight. Here was an inferno, a living hell and it was just a prelude for what was to come.

My very first memory was being taken from my bed by my mother. Parting the blackout curtains she said, 'Look, London's burning.' Who can forget such a sight? To the east there was a dull glow as the East End was set alight. A crimson sky as far as the eye could see. I was far too young to understand the implications of what I was seeing, but it was perceptive and intuitive of my mother to imbue the importance of that moment in my young mind.

To the north in Islington Albert Knight can remember being prevented from going home as an entire row of shops just a few hundred yards from his house had been completely destroyed. Fractured gas mains, furniture and even baths hanging at crazy angles from what a few minutes earlier had been homes. Dead bodies laid out under sheets or tarpaulins are hard for a youngster to forget.

As ever most children looked for positives amongst the devastation. Collecting shrapnel which was still hot acted as a badge of honour for young boys. Girls seeking some distraction from the horrors surrounding them found 'a strange beauty' in the sharpness whilst the colours of the shrapnel changed in the light from silver to pink and blue. A swap market developed with the brass cones of incendiaries being the most prized.

Still the raiders came night after night. Whilst the East End bore the brunt of the early attacks, other areas also endured their share of terror. Robin Burns lived in Cricklewood, his bedroom overlooking school playing fields where ack-ack guns were positioned. His dad was an ARP warden who had been seconded to the heavy lifting rescue unit. Their equipment was absolutely basic, just a set of heavy overalls, a steel helmet, an oilskin cape and respirator to protect them against a gas attack. Being employed in the building trade and having attended a basic first aid course was all that was required to qualify for this dangerous and often distressing job. They had to endure almost daily the most gruesome sights of one's worst nightmare. One of Robin's father's mates, unable to bear any more, committed suicide. Within days he witnessed a death that was to haunt him for the rest of his life. Gently removing plaster and debris he uncovered a young girl who lay in the wreckage of her home. She seemed remarkably unharmed although the dust covering her gave her an almost ghostly air. Opening her eyes she asked in a whisper, 'Am I going to die'? 'Of course not darling' he assured her. Smiling she closed her eyes and never opened them again. Just a glimpse of what was continually playing out across London.

Every night during September the carnage continued. By the end of the month almost six thousand people had been killed and vast tracts lay in smouldering ruins. October did see a relative fall-off in enemy activity. However a full moon on the 15th saw over four hundred bombers target the reeling capital again. Other cities were also being attacked and it was Liverpool which after London suffered most and over a long period extending to January 1942.

On the evening of 14th November 1940 Sheila van de Velde was staying at the Adelphi Hotel in Liverpool prior to leaving for South Africa the following morning. She was the youngest of seven children of a leading figure in the Marconi organisation (later to become its chief executive). Part of a prominent Anglo-Dutch family his work on radar development was considered important enough for him to be transferred to the safety of Cape Town. The problem was getting the family there in one piece. That night Liverpool endured possibly the worst bombing the city had experienced. Her parents and their other three youngest children hid under tables or even in cupboards as the bombs rained down obliterating much of its historic centre. She still vividly remembers the flashes of dazzling light and huge explosions. Astonishingly they all survived although over five hundred Scousers perished that night, with huge numbers more being injured.

The following morning their taxi picked its way through piles of smoking rubble. Police and ARPs continued to dig away in the hope of still finding people alive. The family joined a Union-Castle Line ship which had been converted into a troop carrier. As they left Liverpool docks in convoy they were again attacked by German aircraft, but without sustaining any injuries to passengers or crew. They were to make a circuitous route via Brazil in the hope of avoiding enemy submarines. So young Sheila was lucky to enjoy a happy and privileged stay in South Africa. Back in Liverpool the city continued to endure seemingly endless air-raids. Although as always mass observation contributors moaned about lack of public shelters particularly affecting working class areas. The spirit of Liverpudlians matched their London cousins. Their scaffold humour still remembered and helped sustain them.

There were only three nights during November when London was not bombed. Now it was the ancient city of Coventry that had to endure three nights of horrific attacks, laying waste to its cathedral and medieval centre. All the half timbered buildings and ancient alleys and courtyards swept away in a firestorm. With supremely poor timing Albert Knight's father decided that living in London was too dangerous. He secured a job in an engineering company in Coventry. Within three days of their arrival in their new home they found themselves engulfed in the mayhem and were lucky to survive. A few streets away in Styvechale Avenue, Minny Charles was terrified as the flashes and explosions came ever closer. With hands covering her ears she staggered into a cupboard under the stairs. Even when the noise of falling bombs stopped she was still too frightened to come out. When she finally made her way gingerly to her front door she was unable at first to take in the devastation surrounding her. It was a new horrific landscape of wailing fire engines, buildings still in flames and people staggering about trying to get their bearings. Hers was one of the few houses still standing in a scene from hell. The fires from Coventry were seen as far away as East Langton by Martin van Oppen. He also remembers seeing refugees pushing prams in an attempt to avoid further danger in the days following the Coventry raids.

Back in Edgware my sister remembers the night that four hundred bombers droned northwards. We were lying on a mattress under our Morrison shelter. Ann can remember my mother saying how some other poor devils were going to have their lives wrecked that night. How right she was. She became increasingly alarmed as the bombers came back south having done their work. There were many accounts of the Luftwaffe discharging bombs over suburbia that they had not managed to drop over their intended target. After that night we started spending the evenings in a neighbour's cellar.

Many Londoners brought their evacuated children home just in time to encounter the worst of the Blitz. Ivy Robinson's family opted for rented accommodation in Edmonton, which they reckoned would be far safer than their previous home in East Ham. They were wrong. Her new school had already been bombed so her education was conducted in various neighbours' houses. Still 'moaning Minnie' wailed out her warning each night as the incessant raids continued. She was caught with her mother and sisters in a daylight raid. Planes with German markings flew low overhead and they all dashed for what cover they could find. An elderly man invited them in to his house. Above now Spitfires appeared hunting down the bombers. Despite the danger they all went out into the street again, a feeling of invincibility overtaking them as they cheered as if watching a football match.

It is strange that this feeling appears to have been quite widespread at the time. Probably false bravado prompted by adrenaline and a sense of not being cowered. It is a common theme that those who might have been expected to be brave often folded, whilst the least likely heroes stood tall.

The initial problems encountered with underground stations being opened up was helped with the introduction of additional toilets. Each night people crowded onto the platforms covered in blankets or sleeping bags. Generally the mood was good with sing-songs being a regular feature. Certain spots were particularly prized. Anti-Semitism ran right through British society from the very top. The British continued to be suspicious of all foreigners and people who looked different. So trouble erupted when Jews were accused of always securing the best pitches in the underground.

This was not what Raymond Cooney, a teenager and his younger sister Sylvia found. In his experience the 'Cohens and the Kellys' were great friends and lived alongside each other in complete harmony. They all congregated together in Goodge Street underground station. The surrounding area was home to a large Jewish and Irish population. Their evenings together were remembered as a mixture of violin solos and nostalgic Irish ballads. Perhaps theirs was a natural coming together as the Irish in London still had a reputation for drunkenness and fighting. The stance of the Irish government was also resented and so, in many English minds, different, just like the Jews. Both sets were reckoned to be dubious and 'not doing their bit', this was untrue as numbers of Irish and Jews volunteered for service in the armed forces.

In December the Blitz of the East End continued to rage. Once again a sense of invincibility was noticeable. Jean Picton's grandmother had no intention of skulking indoors. There was a good film on locally and she decided to treat Jean to an afternoon's entertainment. Jean remembers that it was the night that the local celluloid factory was hit from the air, whose flames could be seen for miles around. The film had barely started when the air-raid warning went off. A notice shown on the screen advised everyone to take immediate cover. Ignoring the warning they watched some more of the film before deciding to take a chance and hurry home through the deserted streets. They had not gone far when enemy aircraft appeared flying low right above them. There were sounds of bombs falling not far away. But hunched up as if somehow this protected them, they continued scurrying towards their home. Hearing a high pitched whistle Jean instinctively threw herself to the ground lying on the street. Her gran grabbed her, dragging the young child on her tummy before lying prone on the tarmac, grazing her knees. She pulled the young girl into a doorway as the bomb exploded.

Jean can remember the whole street being lit up as if by floodlights. She said, 'I can remember looking down at my new coat and seeing all the buttons had been scratched right down to the metal'. She started to cry, not out of fright but because her new coat had been ruined.

Still the bombs continued falling on the East End and poor Jean and her family were lucky to escape with their lives. Within weeks of the aborted visit to the cinema as familiar flashes of light and frightening bangs grew closer, her mother pulled her three children into the cupboard under the stairs. She lay across the children hoping to offer them some protection. The lights went out and there was a crashing of glass as their windows were blown out. Eventually it went quiet with only the noise of a fire engine bell sounding as ambulances headed towards them. Miraculously no-one was hurt but granddad suffered just a few bruises after being trapped beneath a fallen wardrobe for some time.

The windows were boarded up but the raids were relentless. Her father, rather like my mother, realised the historic significance of what was going on. During another raid some distance away she remembers him taking her into their back garden and saying, 'Look darling, remember this night.' She did in a strange way, thinking that it was like some wonderland from a Disney film. Whilst her mother begged them to come in, she stood arm in arm with her dad looking skywards. There were flashes of searing light whilst incendiaries fluttered down like candyfloss. Above they could make out planes like giant black eagles swerving to avoid the beam of the searchlights. Now the sound of ack-ack guns was added to the mix. As the explosions grew louder they went inside and despite other narrow squeaks the whole family survived the war.

Shirley Balmer was not evacuated as such, but moved from Hull to Pocklington, a village not far away with her mother and younger brother. It proved a wise move as the bombing of Hull docks intensified. Her father, a policeman, witnessed close up the chaos and death inflicted by the Luftwaffe as he helped in the rescue efforts.

Pocklington was surrounded by farms and so her life in common with others growing up in rural areas was peaceful and relatively uneventful. There was an airbase nearby and she used to watch the huge Wellington bombers flying low overhead with her friends. They would count the planes leaving and then count them back in. Probably because Shirley's mum was still young and very attractive, the family were invited onto the base. A memorable treat was being taken on board a vast empty Wellington. Shirley even remembers being lifted into the pilot's seat surrounded by an array of dials and instruments.

Otherwise life continued at a sedate pace. School during the week and Sunday school on Sunday. The family were Methodists and regular church goers. Her mother had worked in Leeds in the tailoring trade and so Shirley was envied by her friends as her mother took 'make do and mend' to a new level.

Life is unfair and so it proved for children living in cities having to endure heavy bombing raids. These must have been terrifying and yet those who experienced them appear to have come through with no apparent long term effects. The major ports of Southampton, Portsmouth, Glasgow and Belfast all took a beating. So did the major industrial centres of Birmingham which suffered over two thousand deaths. Manchester too endured the attention of the Luftwaffe. Newcastle and Exeter also had many deaths and suffered considerable damage, but it was London that bore the brunt, with over forty thousand deaths, which amounted to more than half the total for Great Britain.

From my discussions it would appear that morale, particularly in the East End, remained generally high despite the devastation. Of course there were those who constantly moaned and complained. There were crooks and those who stole from damaged houses and even from corpses, but generally Cockney humour and bloody mindedness shone through. Morale was helped by periodic visits from Winston Churchill, and also from the King and the Royal Family who remained in London despite Buckingham Palace being hit in 1940.

It was King George VI who perhaps best summed up the overall experience of the Blitz. 'It is not the walls that make the city, but the people within them. The walls of London may be battered, but the spirit of the Londoner stands resolute and undismayed.' For a man not known for his oratory this was a fair summary of those not just living in London, but all across the country who survived the Blitz.

Chapter 7

Food for Thought

The way adults constantly talked about the good times before the war was a source of both frustration and fascination for children, who couldn't imagine a world where everything was available provided you had the money to pay for it. Food, or the current lack of it, was seldom far from people's minds. Talk of exotic fruits like pineapples and bananas had children trying to imagine what they tasted like. They were to have a long wait to experience chocolate eclairs and cream teas, as rationing was introduced and extended until well after the end of the war.

It was in January 1940 that food rationing was introduced to a general feeling of gloom. First on the list was sugar, butter and ham. By March jams, marmalades and preserves had been added, as was syrup, treacle and, importantly, cheese. Shortly afterwards margarine and cooking fats. When tea was also rationed it felt to some that our whole way of life was being undermined. Buff coloured ration books were issued to everyone over school age. Each book contained coupons that could be exchanged for the allowed amount of produce. Ration books had to be registered with a chosen local retailer and it was to this shopkeeper that the housewife had to deal with exclusively when buying for food. Initially the coupons had to be laboriously cut out and returned to the local food office. This was found to be too labour intensive and was replaced by a system that required each coupon to be stamped as proof of purchase.

The authorities were adapting as time passed. Soon milk and eggs were allocated rather than rationed, depending on local supplies and the milk allowance was cut to three pints a week with extra allowed for children and nursing mothers, which was relatively generous compared to other staples. Fruit and vegetables remained off ration which led to an increase in vegetarianism. Often mothers chose to give their allowance to their children. With fish, game and poultry sometimes available it was just possible to maintain a nutritious and healthy diet. However chicken was a rarity for most in a world before the introduction of battery farms. The problem was perpetual shortages. News that the fishmonger was expecting a delivery would lead to instant queues. Queuing became a part of life. Shopping was no longer simple and with few having a fridge it had to be undertaken daily. A national wholemeal loaf was introduced. There was a perception that brown bread was only purchased by those unable to afford white. Today of course many consider wholemeal to be healthier. It certainly looked more appetising than its white alternative that over the war years morphed into a nasty grey colour.

Britain depended on imports, not only to keep industry going but also for its food supplies. The fall of France led to more frequent attacks on our Merchant Navy attempting to cross the Atlantic and these huge losses led to the weekly meat ration being reduced to a miserly 2 ounces per person. Cod liver oil and orange juice were now made available for children. The taste of cod liver oil was reckoned to be foul by most children and led to a daily battle as mothers tried bribery and all their feminine skills in an attempt to get their children to swallow the hated treacle, a ritual which often ended in tears and tantrums.

The government was worried about food waste and started issuing leaflets stating that food was a munition of war with the tag line 'Don't waste'. In addition the Ministry of Food started producing cookery leaflets reflecting the problems housewives were having producing tasty meals. Potatoes featured strongly. Potato pastry was initially recommended before it became obvious that unless it was eaten at once it went rock hard.

Winston Churchill became aware of the rumblings of discontent about food rationing, particularly at the amount of meat allowed. A week's ration was duly presented to him, which he said would be quite enough for him. Unfortunately he was under the illusion that the offering was just for a single meal. By the end of May 1940 rations were already being cut on both sugar and butter and in June the bacon allowance was cut by half to just four ounces. Next a whole range of household goods was added to the list along with furniture and clothes. Bit by bit the screw was being tightened and things that made life acceptable were being withdrawn or restricted. Enemy attacks on docks throughout the country were further adding to the growing list of shortages. With a nod to Christmas the tea and sugar ration was increased for the holiday period.

The noose on supplies continued to tighten and 1941 witnessed the worst period for food shortages. With so much shipping being lost the price of fish soared, forcing the government to introduce price controls.

The public's preoccupation with food was endorsed by the government. The Ministry of Agriculture extolled everyone to 'dig for victory'. Advertisements were placed in national newspapers and women's magazines with the headline 'Whilst the men are away women must dig'. Children were also urged to join their parents in digging and planting vegetables. Preferably cabbages, kale, broccoli and Brussels sprouts to see the family through the bleak winter months. Leaflets were distributed with instructions on how to prepare the ground and plant the vegetable plot. Those with gardens or allotments swung into action. Even bomb sites were cultivated as were the great London parks opposite swanky hotels.

Not to be outdone the Ministry of Food produced their own adverts and tips on bottling and preserving. 'Get pickling' the public were urged, with ideas for pulping and bottling tomatoes. With eggs generally in such short supply the virtue of dried eggs appeared in a range of recipes issued. The results were generally pretty disgusting but they helped fill a hole in young groaning stomachs. The mantra from mothers to their children was simple. 'Eat it up or you will get nothing else'. Wasting food was considered a mortal sin. Tips were given to reproduce left-overs into another meal of sorts. This was underlined by an advert from the Food Ministry headed 'Precious crusts, no scrap'. It advised readers nothing was too small to save. It went further. 'Don't waste a crumb and don't buy bread when potatoes are available'. There were tips on using stale bread. Make rusks for the baby or soak it in milk for a healthy snack.

Commercial organisations were not going to be left on the sidelines. Pyrex ran an advert on how to convert small chops into a man sized meal. Heinz were now unable to offer their full fifty seven varieties, but tinned food still formed an important part of the nation's diet. Their staple of baked beans and tomato soup were still available along with other soups and, of course, corned beef which is still remembered quite fondly by many. Spam, another wartime staple, was also made available and tinned rice pudding still sells well today. Fray Bentos reminded readers that they were still around with their freshly tinned garden peas. Brands that we continue to buy today kept their names in front of the public despite the obvious problems with production. Nescafe manufactured coffee powder but not a taste that would be recognised today. Bovril informed readers about spiced up fish and vegetable dishes, whilst those with a sweeter tooth were told that there was 'nothing like Bird's jelly-de-luxe.'

There was a great emphasis on the need to bring up healthy children. Whilst the mortality rate in children had declined, living conditions in inner cities remained grim and were made worse by the perpetual bombing. Several children's illnesses could be fatal with perhaps diphtheria leading the way. During the war years almost seven million children were vaccinated against the feared disease. The Ministry of Food was busy again giving advice on the vitamins vital for their youngsters. War-time mothers were becoming quite expert in nutrition.

Although most of us would be horrified to be confronted with a war-time diet for year after year, generally few went hungry. It was more a question of quantity rather than quality. Many of us can remember suet puddings which sank like a stone to the pit of the stomach. Steamed roly-poly and treacle sponge were eagerly scoffed by a generation of youngsters. These old sweets still survive and strangely are still featured in some swanky restaurants today.

Thrifty advice was also given about what we today would call recycling. In the 1940s this was a necessity rather than appeasing your social conscience. Nothing was discarded. A use could be found for every off-cut of material. 'Make do and mend' became second nature. It sparked a creative spirit as the unlikeliest items were transformed. Old curtains were made into a dress or coat, with young girls often inheriting these skills from their mothers as ancient Singer sewing machines swung into action. Many birthday and Christmas presents were second-hand or made or re-made by family members.

In 1940 the government set up the first of what was going to be hundreds of British Restaurants. These were originally designed to feed people who had been bombed out, but they came to be remembered by most of us who grew up during that time. They sprang up across the country serving cheap basic meals. They were located in vacated shops, halls or in prefabricated buildings. They are remembered for queues, steamed up windows and arguments with people who lingered too long taking up space while other diners waited for a table. The restaurants rather summed up the British attitude to food at the time. As you moved along the serving hatch a choice of a couple of main courses was normally on offer. The food was not a great deal better than school dinners. Meat, veg and lumpy potatoes served to my memory by the same type of grumpy women we endured at school. Again the puddings tended to be more appetising and all washed down with a strong cup of sugary tea and all for a little over a shilling. Eat it quickly was the rule, not exactly fast food but rather like a petrol station, it was fill up and go. During the war the restaurants consistently served over half a million meals a day.

At home meals followed a familiar pattern. Sunday was the highlight where usually a roast of some kind was served followed by the treat of tinned fruit. My father had laid in a store before the war so solemnly each week a tin was selected. Was it to be pears, apricots or my favourite pineapple. I was quite surprised on seeing my first real pineapple, stupidly thinking they actually grew in chunks. After Sunday lunch it was generally downhill for the rest of the week. A variety of rehashed remains of the meat was served. Shepherds pie on Monday, then perhaps a salad and once in a while a horrible Anglicised curry. For many tea was the evening meal and was likely to be just a hunk of bread and jam washed down with a sugary tea. Despite all the shortages and the plain diet it is generally reckoned that war-time kids grew up healthy and well. Fatty foods like suet puddings did not produce fat or obese children. This may well be due to the fact that children walked everywhere. If we weren't walking we were riding bikes. It was a young army constantly on the move. Walking miles to school, walking to the shops with mum, cycling, roller-skating, never still, burning off the calories. To a modern audience the upbringing of children in the 1940s must seem strange and possibly even deprived. Absent fathers, dodging bombs, surrounded by adults worried about the outcome of the war and yet...

Margaret Woodcock's war was very different from all the others mentioned in this book. She was not from a wealthy country background or indeed someone brought up in a tied cottage. She was not from a deprived slum or from the relative comfort of leafy suburbs. Margaret along with her elder sister Beth were the granddaughters of Ernest Woodcock who started a drapery store in Kettering in 1894. By the 1930s it had grown into a fully fledged department store and was run by their father. The store survived into the 1960s when central buying left stores like Woodcock's being unable to compete. During the war years though it still held sway in Kettering, occupying a substantial three-storey building in Gold Street with numerous departments and selling a wide range of products.

The family lived in a sizeable eight-bedroomed town house where, to their mother's consternation, they had over twenty Canadian troops billeted on them for a while. The girls often visited the store. It still sold linens, fabrics and haberdashery together with a full fashion department with hats and handbags on offer. The store claimed it could serve its customers from cradle to the grave, having both a baby department and even an undertaking business. This must have given the family a very comfortable standard of living and yet the girls were never allowed to be aware of this. Their upbringing, like all who have contributed to this book, was understated having the value of money drummed into them. As kids we never saw the social differences that so consumed adults. All we ever wanted at that time was our next meal and then to rush out and play and enjoy ourselves.

Chapter 8

Fun and Games

The lack of new toys being manufactured or imported during the war was compensated for by whole new playgrounds being opened up for many town and city kids. Although really dangerous bomb sites were boarded up this left many with easy access. Ropes were attached to exposed beams and lintels in order to enable scruffy kids to clamber up their pretend castles. Ignoring the tragedy of ruined homes, casualties and even deaths, the opportunities were too good to ignore despite the warnings of parents and neighbours. Soon flowers long absent from the area stated appearing, as did butterflies and ladybirds. Some city children started taking an interest in nature for the first time. Meanwhile many of their country cousins were spending their spare time bird watching and unfortunately collecting birds' eggs. Despite this many grew up with a profound love and knowledge of the natural life all around them.

With so little traffic on the roads town and suburban children were often left free to play football or cricket in the street. The problem, particularly as the war wore on, was the lack of balls to play with. Bald tennis balls often had to be used for both games as leather cricket balls were seldom seen and the composition replacements were an unsatisfactory substitute.

Most mothers encouraged their children to get out from under their feet soon after breakfast. Fresh air was good for them and so outdoor activities thrived. For those old enough, having a bike was a passport to freedom. I would go to Scratch Woods or Stanmore Common with friends for the whole day. It was a lengthy ride to get there but the reward was being able to charge down deserted paths pretending to be knights in armour. There was less worry then about traffic and we were told repeatedly not to talk to strangers.

Although boys and girls tended to play separately, certain ancient games drew them together. Hopscotch can be traced back to Roman times and over the centuries armies have used the game to improve the fitness and balance of their fighting men. Requiring only a stretch of road where the court can be chalked out, it was a game that kept children engaged for hours. Tag has also been played for centuries and at my school it normally ended up in a kiss-chase. Young boys always claimed that they wanted nothing to do with girls, but even at a very young age an attraction (no matter how strongly denied) existed.

The one skill that few boys were able to compete with the girls was skipping. Either in pairs or singly, many girls were capable of routines that would not have looked out of place on stage. Some boys made passable efforts but most were clumsy and lacking the agility needed and having been humiliated they grumbled that skipping was only for cissies, so few continued. Children hate above all else being considered an outsider.

It is interesting how some of the most basic fears are played out in ancient games still undertaken today. There is a basic desire to be scared or frightened, but not too much. So chasing games like 'who's afraid of the big bad wolf' are passed down through the generations. 'Hide and seek' is another that shows no sign of being sidelined. Another ancient throwback, spinning tops, was still popular during the war and here again girls were often more successful than the boys, probably because more of them were patient and didn't expect instant success. Some yo-yos had also been handed down by previous generations and skill and a steady hand were needed to keep the motion going.

Marbles were much prized as none were currently being manufactured. Again the advantage of this ancient game was that it could be played almost anywhere. Rough ground, even gutters were a sufficient surface for battle to commence.

Perhaps even more prized than marbles were cigarette cards. Whilst most adults continued to puff away on cigarettes, the manufacturers had stopped printing cards. Their scarcity added to their appeal. Collecting of whatever interests attracts children from a young age. The only way to increase your collection of cards required an element of risk. Whilst some cigarette cards were amicably exchanged, most were won or lost playing flickers. There were two basic variants of this game and where sizeable quantities were involved large noisy crowds formed. The game where you had to cover your opponent's card to claim it required a certain skill, but the big gains and losses were had in a variant of the game. Here the two rivals lined up an equal number of cards each against a wall. Then taking it in turns they tried to knock their opponent's card down by flicking a missile card. To cheers and groans collections were either swollen or depleted.

During the summer holidays and when the sun was shining it was time for a visit to the swimming baths. Most of these were council owned and were often open-air. Avoiding the show-offs descending from the diving boards, it was time to gently lower yourself into the water and find a space. Whilst the teenagers sunbathed the children splashed around, the youngest supported by rubber armbands. When the weather cooled the baths tended to be deserted apart from the real enthusiasts.

Roller skating rinks had become very popular during the 1930s but most of these had closed down with the outbreak of war. The skates containing ball-bearings were prized as you sped along the pavements. Unfortunately the ones I had were made of such flimsy metal that they tended to fold once I put my weight on them as I languished behind most of my friends.

Of course for much of the year bad weather or shortened days required us to create our enjoyment indoors. Here once more the interests of boys and girls tended to be different. It was still an age where children were guided towards traditional recreation for the different sexes. For example dolls for girls and train sets for boys. Of course many girls went through a 'tomboy phase' annoyed by what they saw as being sidelined from really exciting activities. Resented at first, these energetic girls were often grudgingly accepted as being all right with the proviso 'for a girl'.

In a time before such things were judged offensive many dolls were brown skinned and gollywogs considered particularly cuddly. My sister had a doll with blue eyes which opened and closed depending on the angle it was held. As with the vast majority of toys most of these traditional dolls had been handed down or were bought second hand.

Possibly the most coveted equivalent for boys was toy soldiers. Produced before the war they were cast in fine detail. Scarlet tunics, bearskin hats and even guardsmen mounted on gleaming black horses. There were Scottish regimental kilts and all reproduced in fine detail. Made of tin or some other metal, they would be banned today as being unsafe and poisonous, but we didn't know this and how we longed to own some but once more they were in short supply and too expensive for most.

For miserable rainy days it was time to bring out the stamp album. My father had a friend who travelled widely abroad and for a time he sent me stamps from the country he had been visiting. Mostly European, the French stamps were rather plain and boring, but the pride of my collection came from Germany. Stamps bearing Hitler's image and even better those with the swastika were much envied by my friends. The most spectacular however came from Tanganyika with the image of a giraffe. I had a very eccentric great uncle who lived in Broadstairs whom we occasionally visited. He was always dressed in a brocade smoking jacket and wore a fez on his head. He boasted that his stamp collection was second only to the King's. It certainly was vast, contained in numerous leather bound albums. I wonder where that collection is now. He also had an enormous collection of exotic butterflies all neatly skewered and housed in glass cabinets.

My grandmother taught me to play cards almost before I could read. Her favourite was progressive rummy which at least taught me to count. The games were very competitive. She didn't like losing and would sometimes cheat. She was great. I sensed in her a naughtiness that was still apparent in her eighties. Sitting with her for hours we progressed on to solo-whist and pontoon. There was another horse racing card game played with a dice that occupied the whole family for hours.

Most young boys had a fascination with trains. This was probably because before air travel became commonplace the train station was a major source of excitement. It was often the start of a journey into the unknown. Mainline stations crackled with activity. Porters with luggage piled high on barrows waited hand outstretched for a tip, having heaved the cases onto the luggage rack. The vast steam engine acted as if alive, hissing and grumbling as the fire in the cab was stoked. Then as the guard waved his green flag the engine gasped and wheezed into a roar, and to a background of smoke and soot the journey began.

This preoccupation with trains manifested itself in the prized possession of a train set. Bedrooms and even living rooms were given over to various types and formations. Even sisters became caught up in the excitement. Some of the electric sets were really sophisticated with stations and tunnels adding to the authenticity. Even those relying on old clockwork versions were able to get hours of fun even though the track only went round in circles.

For many youngsters the fascination with trains extended to train spotting. They would stand for hours on exposed platforms solemnly recording or tracing the locomotives as they sped by. Those of us not so intrigued considered the train spotters rather boring and a bit weird. This interest in recording transport extended to buses. In London each double or single decker red bus had its own individual number printed on the side of the cab. So it was that trains and buses were added to stamp and coin collecting. This interest in collecting, albeit in a wider choice of subjects, obviously lurks deep in many of us.

For the engineers and builders of the future Meccano helped hone their practical skills. From small kits it was possible to build up a huge collection of parts that would enable a wide range of projects to be undertaken. Meccano can be likened to an early form of Lego but using metal rather than plastic. Production was halted in 1942 as the material they were using was required for the war effort. Along with other toys being in such short supply the cost of second hand goods soared, particularly with the approach of Christmas.

Board games were also extremely popular as many involved several players. Games that could be played by the whole family. It is reckoned that you can tell a person's character by the way they play Monopoly. Certainly it often seemed to define children. You had the cautious ones who bought the utilities like the electric company or perhaps the stations. At the other end of the scale were the heroic optimists drawn to the high life of Park Lane and Mayfair before finding themselves with no money to develop the sites. Games could run into several hours and often involved toxic rows. It was frequently the quiet accumulator of the medium priced properties like Vine Street or Fleet Street who emerged the winners. Looking back on my own experiences with the game it is fascinating that those traits spotted in childhood tended to carry on as they grew older. The choice of token for the players also tended to tell a story. Watch out for those who chose the top hat who wanted to become the future captains of industry as opposed to those who chose the racing car who tended to be the supreme optimists.

At home we had a games set that offered three choices. Ludo could be played by up to four participants and was a game relying on the roll of the dice, in a sense a more sophisticated form of snakes and ladders as you tried to get your four tokens home before your opponents. Once again the game could take a long time to complete as the dice obstinately refused to come up with the number you required. The inside section of our games board was given over to a steeplechase game, which again depended on the roll of the dice, but the game we played most was draughts. The combinations were endless and the game gave a grounding for youngsters into the fascinating world of chess.

Being invited to a friend's birthday party was generally a highlight of a child's year. At least to start with. It frequently ended in tears and invariably one poor child being sick over the carpet. It was all just too exciting. All those games with parents proudly looking on. All those jam sandwiches with jelly and evaporated milk to follow. Often a fatal combination. Tears and tantrums before musical chairs had finished. Boys being too rough and pushing girls much smaller than them aside. A telling-off from mum and knowing looks from other parents. The game eventually being awarded to a girl to cries of 'unfair' and generally boorish behaviour from the boys.

Moving on to 'pinning the tail on the donkey' does not improve matters as the girls appear to have far greater spatial awareness. Behaviour continues to deteriorate and children are being instructed to apologise to the lady of the house who is already regretting being drawn in to hosting the party by her children. The chances are that within a week it will turn out that one of the children has chicken pox or measles and one by one all the party-goers succumb.

All these games and hobbies help form the child as they head towards those difficult teenage years. The parties hopefully helping in the social interaction required for a happy life. More than ever for kids growing up to a background of war, these acted as a distraction from the disruption and chaos impacting so many of their lives.

Chapter 9

Street Life

What goes on behind other people's closed doors remains a mystery to us, but just outside much of the theatre of life is played out. From village lane to city centre street there is always something of interest going on. The streets of war-time Britain were very different from those of today even allowing for the bomb damage in many city centres.

There were far less cars on the roads partly replaced by an increase in military traffic. Horses were still widely used even in central London where they struggled against a tide of buses, trams and lorries. In city centres dray horses were still often used to deliver barrels of beer to the local pubs. In central London the former stables have been converted into fashionable mews houses which now sell at eye watering prices.

Street markets are part of Britain's heritage and in a time of acute shortages they flourished. They attracted not only bargain hunters but pickpockets and all manner of rogues such as traders who furtively opened a suitcase offering all sorts of goods which were normally difficult to buy. Many would claim their merchandise was 'knocked off' to encourage customers to buy before the police arrived. This claim was often untrue and the goods were just faulty but the spiv always disappeared before the punter found that they had been conned.

Another favourite where the unwary lost out was the three card trick often known as 'find' or 'chase the lady'. Three cards would be laid out on the road. The cards were laid face down having first been shown to the small crowd gathered round. There was a King, Jack and Queen. Money was staked on the card thought to be the Queen. A stooge seemingly won consistently, drawing in unsuspecting members of the public. Using sleight of hand the winning bets dried up and the card-sharps melted into the crowd before onlookers turned nasty or the law arrived.

Petticoat Lane in Spitalfields is one of London's oldest and most famous markets which continued as noisily as ever amidst the devastation caused by bombing. Jean Sporle was a regular visitor to Hammersmith market with her mother who worked in a local armaments factory. Jean loved the excitement and buzz of the place where the stallholders shouted out their wares and this was the scene that was replicated throughout the country.

In more rural areas sleepy market towns sprung into life on market day. In Market Harborough, whilst most cattle and sheep were driven to market, some continued to be guided by drovers from the surrounding villages. It was a chance for farmers to get together and chat as the animals were auctioned off. The town's numerous pubs were soon filled to capacity. Stalls were set up in the town square offering fruit and vegetables along with second hand clothing, antiques and knick-knacks. Horses, some with carts, were tethered to hitching posts and it was still possible to see an old shepherd dressed in his traditional white smock. This was a scene that had hardly changed in centuries except for the recent addition of men in military uniforms who were joined later in the war by groups of slightly bemused GIs. They were often accompanied by smug looking young women whilst the young locals glowered at the fickleness of the girls.

During the winter it was darkness that most affected everyone's lives. Children would sometimes go to school in the dark and return as the dusk fell. Familiar streets became forests of uncertainty as people groped their way home. People passed like ghosts listening out for traffic that appeared with little warning. In rural areas many signposts were taken down in an attempt to confuse any Germans who may have found their way to Britain, further complicating travel.

With so few people able to drive cars due to petrol rationing public transport became a vital part of keeping the country functioning. In the major cities a combination of buses, trams and trolley-buses attempted to keep to their timetables despite the regular disruption caused by bombing. In London the famous red buses growled their way across the capital, a reassuring sight adding a little normality to these exceptional times. The buses looked rather different to those now in service. To reach the upper deck the passenger had to negotiate an outside staircase open to the elements. The conductor would issue tickets of a different colour depending on the length of the journey. The tickets were kept in a wooden clipboard and were franked with a ping when placed in a metal machine worn by the conductor, that punched a hole in the ticket to prove payment. Wartime conditions did not inhibit advertisers and every available space on the exterior of the bus was covered, with more exhibited inside in an attempt to influence the captive audience.

Buses had a real advantage over trams in wartime conditions, being able to re-route if confronted with bomb damage. For trams run on immovable lines this option was not available, thus causing much disruption during the Blitz. Trams were operational throughout the country from Glasgow to Birkenhead and down to Gloucester. Developed from horse-drawn trams in the mid-nineteenth century, they eventually converted to electricity and were an important part of our transport system. Their limitations were emphasised in Bristol in 1941 when a severe raid permanently closed the city's system down to be replaced by buses.

Trolley-buses were introduced in 1911 in Leeds and Bradford. Like trams, although popular for many years, they were hampered by inflexibility. If a car broke down in their path it was difficult for the bus to continue. Frequent power cuts during the war could leave their passengers stranded. Gradually they were finally withdrawn from service in 1972.

A feature of street life during the war was the number of hawkers and tradesmen who regularly visited. Tally-men were a common sight in working class areas. A small amount was collected each week towards big ticket items which could not be afforded normally. Jean Sporle remembers these visits and also from the rent collector who many tried to avoid, but they all had to pay up eventually or risk a visit from the bailiff.

Less threatening were the visits of the knife-grinder. The operators were often gypsies. They usually had a wheel attachment to their pedal bike and children used to gather round to watch the sparks fly as the knives or scissors were honed to razor sharpness. The cry of the rag and bone man could be heard well before he arrived, allowing plenty of time for old clothes and bits of unwanted household goods to be loaded onto his horse-drawn cart. Rat catchers operated in both town and country with varying success. Ingenious rat traps were devised and some even came with a prize cat or terriers.

Milk was almost exclusively delivered by horse-drawn carts. Shirley Balmer, living just outside Hull, remembers daily visits. The milk was ladled out from huge churns. My sister Ann was standing in for me one day on the milk round when she witnessed a robbery. A man snatched an old lady's handbag and ran off with it. Jack, our milkman friend, leapt down from the milk cart and gave chase. Despite his tuberculosis he was fit enough to catch the thief and pinion him to the ground. A neighbour hearing the commotion rang the police. For over ten minutes Jack held the thief down whilst my sister tried to control the horse unsettled by the shouting. Eventually the thief was taken off in a police car and Jack was commended for his citizen's arrest.

Our street markets continue to connect us with our past. They project vibrancy and excitement as successive generations try to seek out bargains.

Chapter 10

'Goodnight children everywhere'

Over four million children tuned into Children's Hour each night at five o'clock. It had started way back in 1922 and became essential listening during the war years. It offered a mix of features on subjects ranging from history and science to wildlife and classical music. Mostly it was the plays and serials that had the most appeal with children hurrying home from school or playing in order not to miss the next episode. For Derek McCulloch, the main presenter: 'nothing but the best is good enough for children'. Good to his word the programmes were always produced to the highest standards avoiding being patronising to their audience. McCulloch sought to 'stimulate their imaginations, direct their reading, encourage their various interests, widen their outlook and inculcate the Christian virtues of love of God and their neighbours'. Maybe not patronising but certainly a rather moralistic approach which would probably be somewhat ridiculed today. To understand this ethos we need to know more about this man who is so fondly remembered by a whole generation as Uncle Mac.

It was Derek McCulloch's misfortune to have been born in 1897, ensuring that he was going to be caught up in the horrors of the Great War. As a nineteen year old he was serving in the Middlesex regiment on the Somme. He was shot in the face, losing his right eye and sustaining further shrapnel wounds. Despite this he continued to serve firstly in the Green Howards before transferring to the Royal Flying Corps. Back in Britain he joined the BBC in 1926 initially as an announcer. Plagued by bad health caused by his injuries, including having a bullet removed from his lung, he joined Children's Hour in 1929, and years later he was promoted to take charge of children's output for the BBC. The poor man was then involved in a road accident resulting in him losing a leg. This was relevant as his suffering appeared to give him a gentle vulnerability that appealed to children. He really was that kind uncle whom so many still remember today.

The attraction of Children's Hour for youngsters was underlined by Elizabeth Davies who was living in Northampton. She would run home from school with her younger brother, both eager not to miss the start of the programme. Her father, who had seen active service in the Great War, was now a special constable. In winter there was always a fire burning and cakes or biscuits magicked somehow by her mother from the sparse ration allowance. For Betty, now in her nineties, this scene of a warm loving home, listening to Children's Hour epitomises her happy childhood.

It is music that best evokes memories and it was William Walton's 'Façade' that introduced the very popular series 'Said the Cat to the Dog' featuring Mumpty the cat and Peckham the dog who lived with the Jackson family. The plays were written by William Armstrong involving mum and dad Jackson and their children Diana and Ronnie. Like so many of the Children's Hour productions it was brought to life by the excellence of the cast that included the narrator Lewis Stringer.

Music again prompted memories of another classic broadcast series. Ballet Shoes was based on the book by Noel Streatfeild written in 1936. It featured music by the Italian composer Ermanno Wolf-Ferrari. Despite its great popularity with girls, Ballet Shoes was dwarfed by the huge success of Toytown. The series was first broadcast back in 1929, but continued to be adapted right through until Children's Hour was withdrawn in the 1960s. There were over thirty plays, a cast of characters including Larry the Lamb, the Mayor and Mister Growser. Larry the Lamb was played by Derek McCulloch (uncle Mac) with many other notable actors featured over the years. These included Norman Shelley who played the leading role of Dennis the dachshund, in Toytown. Most memorably he also played the title role of Winnie the Pooh in the BBC's adaptation of the book by A.A. Milne.

Other actors who appeared regularly on Children's Hour and who went on to achieve national fame included Violet Carson and Wilfred Pickles. Years later Violet Carson played the grumpy Ena Sharples in Coronation Street and became one of the most recognisable faces on television. Wilfred Pickles, whose appointment as a BBC announcer had caused controversy at the time, went on to host the extremely popular Have a Go programme in 1946. It was his Yorkshire accent that upset some senior figures at the BBC who wanted to keep to their perception of 'speaking proper'. In a time when newsreaders wore dinner jackets to speak to the nation, there was a fear of standards slipping generally, but not at the BBC.

The output of children's programmes continued to expand. It was impossible to ignore the demand which grew even larger at weekends when adults joined their children listening in. Talks from experts on science and the environment proved popular, whilst music was largely confined to the lighter classics. However it was drama that continued to draw the largest audiences, particularly serials with each new episode being eagerly anticipated.

David Davis had a perfect voice for story-telling. He joined Children's Hour in 1935 and soon became known as 'uncle David'. His popularity was second only to uncle Mac with his soft welcoming voice. His reading of stories like Wind in the Willows and Black Beauty were classics of their type. Recognised as such an influential figure in so many children's lives, he appeared on Desert Island Discs in August 1970.

Remembered with such affection by those who were children at the time, today's society may well take a different view. Certainly Children's Hour projected what was essentially a middle class, middle brow view of how children should be encouraged to develop. It was an attempt by the BBC to guide their young listeners to be polite and caring, but also inquisitive. Despite its undoubted manipulation millions of children tuned in each afternoon at five o'clock with a sense of anticipation. Radio rather than television allows the listener to interpret and imagine the story being told. Together with reading it allowed a whole generation growing up in extraordinary times to give flight to their imagination.

Children's Hour offered stability and familiarity in a world made mad by adults. Few would not deny having a lump in their throats if they listened again to uncle Mac saying: 'goodnight children' then after a slight pause and said with emphasis 'everywhere'.

Chapter 11

Saturday Morning Pictures

Take any town or city in the 1940s on a Saturday morning and you would have witnessed a strange phenomenon. It was as if an invisible pied-piper was drawing children from every quarter. Boys and girls aged from about six to young teenagers all heading in one direction, to the local cinema. Earlier when most of them had been built they were known as picture palaces and it is easy to see why. Going to 'the pictures' was a chance to escape and enter a sort of wonderland.

Although many of the buildings were beginning to look rather faded and in need of decoration, this passed us youngsters by as we joined the queue for our two hours of entertainment. For this morning only there was no difference in the admission price. A few pence gained entry and you were then guided into the stalls or the circle on the first floor. Before the performance began there was a huge wave of excited conversation and unruly behaviour. Many clutched a bag of sweets, the last of the week's ration. Then to cheers the house lights were lowered.

The programme was changed each week but the format remained very much the same. The kids were offered a mixture of old silent films, cartoons, a cowboys and indians film and a serial. Frequent breaks in a film reel were greeted with howls of derision, but once the show continued you could hear a pin drop, but not for long for audience participation was part of the Saturday experience. Howls of laughter for Laurel and Hardy whilst we never tired of Harold Lloyd hanging on to the hands of a giant skyscraper clock. The film had been made in the early 1920s, but classic silent comedy never seems to age. Often words get in the way.

Certainly one of the favourite features for boys was Roy Rogers 'king of the cowboys' and his horse Trigger. Rogers made over one hundred films all featuring gun battles and rearing horses charging across barren countryside. All of this, the cartoons, the comedy and the thrill and excitement of the westerns allowed this scruffy army of kids to escape and light their imaginations. Once they left the make believe world of the cinema it was back to reality. A dull world of bombs, missing dads and rationing. On the way home we imagined it was us riding a grey horse chasing the baddies. We were lucky though because we were the generation that enjoyed a golden age of children's films brought to us by the genius of Walt Disney.

There are certain landmarks in our lives that we tend to remember forever. The first date with the one we love or maybe our first day at school. Along with those land marks for many of us would be the first film we saw at a cinema. The anticipation, the seeming vastness of the auditorium, the velvet covered tip-up seats.

Perhaps we had already seen some cartoon shows, including the wonderful Mickey Mouse or the outrageous Donald Duck, but that first feature film is what remains vividly in our minds. Although Snow White and the Seven Dwarfs had been released before the war it was still on general release in the 1940s and was an initial introduction to the magic of the cinema for countless children of that generation, including Arthur Price-Jones who remembers being taken by his mother to the Regal cinema in Oswestry.

Despite the success of early cartoons Walt Disney took a huge risk in the making of Snow White with production costs ballooning to over a million dollars. Would audiences really be drawn into a full length feature film headed by cartoon characters rather than known movie stars? Teams of animators were recruited by the studio to create a magical setting for the film that cleverly mixed drama, humour and pathos and for the first time managed to involve the audience's emotions with cartoon characters as if they were real. From the opening sequence the viewer is drawn into a fantasy world and an array of memorable characters. Even viewed through today's cynical eye you feel involved. You want to boo Snow White's wicked stepmother and laugh at the antics of the dwarfs (there is some criticism today that the dwarfs in the film reinforce the stereotyping of dwarfism). However audiences continued to be enthralled by the sheer beauty on the screen. It is as if we are children again seeing the film for the first time.

Perhaps the greatest breakthrough was Disney's ability to accurately synchronise the speech of the characters to the soundtrack on screen. This involved countless thousands of illustrations being individually drawn. A combination of the creative and technical, achieving a standard never reached before. A full length feature cartoon that created a template for what was to follow. Another important development in Disney films was his use of music to help create the atmosphere he was seeking.

In Snow White her jealous stepmother, the wicked princess, asks 'mirror, mirror on the wall, who's the fairest one of all'. Across cinemas children begin to reach for their handkerchiefs as Snow White appears to die after eating a poisonous apple given to her by the princess disguised as an old hag. The spell can only be reversed by a kiss from a prince. Luckily one turns up and all is well. It all sounds very hammy but somehow Disney pulls it off. All of a youngster's emotions are taxed and the film and the breathtaking scenery draws you in. Although it was not the first film seen by Jean Sporle, Snow White remains a favourite. Sitting all those years ago with her mother in the Commodore cinema in Hammersmith, she was swept into a magical make-believe world so different from the grey, grim reality outside, but Walt Disney was now planning another leap in the dark by seeking to further expand and develop a magical world, but one once again involving huge financial risk.

Initially planned to be a vehicle for Mickey Mouse (whose popularity had been declining), to star in a musical animation of 'The Sorcerer's Apprentice' it was extended into a full length feature film. Fantasia cost even more to produce than Snow White and presented a far greater risk. Would the public really buy into a film featuring classical rather than popular music? For over two hours you are transported on an extraordinary journey with animated figures and soaring music, all intertwined with astonishing imagery. This was a massive departure with music normally only heard on records or in the concert hall suddenly now enveloping the audience in cinemas. This was a film that had a profound and permanent effect on some youngsters, introducing them to a world of serious music all wrapped up in an unforgettable visual landscape. This was certainly true of Michael Goddard who saw Fantasia at the Cameo cinema in Silver Street, Leicester. He went on to develop a life-long love of serious music becoming a very talented pianist and organist, whilst his sister Erica became a professional musician and soloist.

The film revolved around eight symphonies with Leopold Stokowski conducting the Philadelphia orchestra. This was one time when you certainly did not want to listen to the music with your eyes shut. The start of the film was strangely conventional considering what was to follow. There are vague shadows of musicians tuning their instruments as the theatre lights are dimmed. The compère Deems Taylor takes to the rostrum to introduce the show. He explains it is to be a 'representation of design and pictures and stories'. This is followed by the shadow of Leopold Stokowski as he ascends the podium and the concert begins. But this is not like any concert anyone has witnessed before.

First is Bach's Toccata and Fugue. To some this may appear pretty boring but it is transformed by brilliant colours shifting and merging, whilst wispy figures join in space with sprays of falling stars. The effect is almost mesmeric but it sets the tone for the rest of the performance. The film continued in the same rather strange way with the compère introducing Tchaikovsky's Nutcracker Suite. To the background of the stirring music shimmering fairies place dewdrops on cobwebs, this is followed by animated Chinese mushrooms dancing in time to the music. There are battles of prehistoric animals in Stravinsky's Rite of Spring and we are not denied the presence of Mickey Mouse who appears in The Sorcerer's Apprentice. Stranger still is the satirical version of Dance of the Hours performed by a troop of hippos and elephants. The effects continue to bewilder for the images Disney produces are so weird that today people might suppose they had been imagined by someone either drunk or stoned. This was never more apparent than in the section to form the background for Mussorgsky's Night on Bald Mountain. Many young children were terrified by the assortment of ghouls, imps and skeletons swirling round the ominous darkness of the mountain.

Walt Disney described Fantasia as an experiment, but many thought it to be his ultimate masterpiece. There were also critics who felt that although the film had trivialised great music, this was marginalised by the fantastical imagery conjured up by his animators and technicians. Technicolour was particularly suited for cartoons and had been used previously by Disney, but was developed further to such effect in Fantasia. It was also used in another iconic children's film The Wizard of Oz.

This was MGM's response to the huge success of Snow White. Dorothy (played by Judy Garland) and her little dog Toto are whisked away to the magical land of Oz during a hurricane in her home town of Kansas. Along the yellow brick road that leads to the emerald city she encounters the scarecrow who lacks a brain, the tin man who lacks a heart and the lion who lacks courage. Once again a make believe world is created. The film has a wonderful mixture of music, pathos, comedy and special effects. Although youngsters take it at face value, many subsequent interpretations have been suggested by adults. Certainly if you listen carefully to Judy Garland singing 'Somewhere over the Rainbow' you can sense her own unhappiness at the time of the recording. It was her undoubted vulnerability that added to her performance. The film appealed to a wide range of ages. Was it just a wonderful film or did it carry some deeper meaning? Maybe, but Hollywood moguls are normally fixated on one thing only - profit. For them 'Somewhere over the Rainbow' was firmly lodged in their bank account. If people wanted to look for some deeper meaning that was fine if it put bums on seats.

Some older children were allowed to accompany their parents to another technicolour blockbuster, still on release in the early 1940s – Gone with the Wind. This epic historical romance based on the book by Margaret Mitchell had no hidden meaning. It was just a straight forward story brilliantly told which still enchants children today. Despite this being a golden time for the film industry it was impossible to ignore Walt Disney and his restless ambition to create new, innovative, full length feature cartoons. In Pinocchio he again broke new ground with the wooden puppet who longed to be a boy. The film continued to draw children into a fantasy world enlivened by music that still remains popular today. In 1942 he produced Bambi, a classic that pulled at the heartstrings of every child watching it.

Initially Bambi was not a great box office success as it was thought to be too upsetting for young children. It certainly was, but it is still remembered by every child who saw it at the time. Interestingly, just like the classic silent comedy films, Bambi is still relevant to youngsters today as they too burst into tears as Bambi's mother is shot and dies. Originally she was seen on screen being killed but later Disney was persuaded to withdraw this scene. Once again it is Disney's unique ability to engage his audience (including adults) in the story unfolding on screen. Bambi is so powerful because it highlights the passage from an idyllic childhood and the often painful route to adulthood. In times of war it seemed particularly relevant as children grappled with the possible loss of a parent and the sadness to be slowly overcome.

On a purely entertainment level Bambi continues to delight and shock in equal measure. The wonderful forest scenes as Bambi makes friends with the old owl, Thumper the rabbit and a skunk called Flower. Bambi's father is a proud antlered deer referred to as the prince of the forest, but as winter draws in the dangers for Bambi increase. His mother takes him foraging for food in a barren, snow covered landscape. They spot the first sign of spring grass breaking through the frozen ground just as they hear the arrival of huntsmen and their frightening, black snarling dogs, but as they run for their lives a single shot rings out. Despite not discovering his mother on screen it is made clear that she is dead. At this point in cinemas throughout the world handkerchiefs were handed to weeping children. Disney was following an old tradition where children's stories and rhymes often involved death. Of course the film demands a happy ending and the final shots are of a fully grown Bambi, now sporting impressive antlers. He stands on a rockface looking down as the new prince of the forest.

So it was that 'going to the pictures' influenced the children of the 1940s. It introduced them to a feast of laughter, excitement and drama. Paul McCartney attributed his interest in animal rights to seeing Bambi as a child. Dumbo had also been another great success for the Disney studio which had now grown enormously as the dollars continued to roll in.

Times have changed so much. Many children today have never visited a cinema, watching films instead on a tablet or some other device. Saturday pictures is just a memory, a thing of the past. It is now a rarity for children to form an entire audience without adults. A unique experience missed.

Reading is also in decline with children today whereas eighty years ago it was a major activity. It allowed children to develop their interests and spark their imagination. The big question was did your parents allow you to read comics or were they banned?

Chapter 12

Desperate Dan and Pals

It was a middle class thing. A feeling that comics were bad for children. It was no use, these undoubtedly well meaning people were fighting a losing cause. By the beginning of the war circulation for children's comics soared. Perhaps it was the new rather irreverent tone adopted by the Beano and the Dandy that upset some adults but appealed so much to children. Not all adults objected as young Vicky Bent had to race to the letterbox in an attempt to be able to read the Beano before her father bagged it.

Children's comics have enjoyed a long history. Chips had been published since the time of the Boer war and was still popular. Others like Jester and the Rainbow had been in circulation since the Great War. It was the appearance of the Dandy and the Beano published by D.C. Thomson in Dundee that galvanised the market and threatened the existence of its more traditional rivals.

With the outbreak of war the comic industry started to adopt a very patriotic approach, seldom missing an opportunity to have a dig at Hitler and his cronies. The Dandy featured Addie and Hermy 'the nasty Nazis', whilst the Beano created 'Musso the Wop'. Even the more traditional Jester comic introduced 'Artful Adolf', all floppy hair and demonic stare. Still selling for only a penny the Jester was the comic that boasted that they were 'the paper of the black-out' Their best known characters were Basil and Bert, our very private detectives. Some comic characters have survived in the public's consciousness long after the demise of the publication that launched them. 'Weary Willie and Tired Tim' is still a term used today but Chips finally closed in 1953. Knock-out was the magnet comic featuring Billy Bunter 'the fattest schoolboy on earth'. Like all the comics at the time Billy Bunter's escapades were told through a series of illustrations with speech bubbles to move the story along. Perhaps because of Bunter's popularity Knock-out felt able to charge a hefty threepence for an edition that came out each Wednesday. The

Rainbow was another old established comic whose headline character was Tiger Tim supported by the Bruin boys. Having survived from 1914 the comic was amalgamated with Tiger Tim's weekly in 1940.

It was really the 1950s before publishers realised the full potential for girls' comics. Tiny Tots would probably have appealed to them but this was incorporated into the Sunbeam in 1940. By then the D.C. Thomson stable of publications had caught the imagination of the young that left their rivals scrambling to find an answer to this newcomer who managed to introduce a whole raft of characters still fondly remembered today. The Dandy started publication in December 1937 with the first edition of the Beano being released the following year. From then on they were issued on alternate weeks throughout the 1940s and beyond. The success of a family owned publisher based in Dundee can be attributed to their ability in creating such outstanding and memorable characters. For decades Korky the Cat occupied the front page of the Dandy. Felix the Cat had been a huge cartoon success before the arrival of Mickey Mouse. James Crichton, Korky's original artist was obviously influenced by Disney characters in producing an instantly recognisable figure to appear on the most important page of the comic. Korky came to be synonymous with the Dandy, despite them introducing other comic strip characters that won even more acclaim later.

First amongst these must rank the cow-pie eating Desperate Dan. Billed as the world's strongest man, he appears bursting out of his red shirt and blue trousers. He sports a few days stubble on his chin, whilst his huge head features a battered old hat. Somehow this strange invention of a character struck an instant cord with children. With food being so scarce during the war it was a constant source of interest for youngsters, and often the final illustration in both the Dandy and the Beano featured the characters getting stuck into a plate piled with food.

On the few occasions Korky did not dominate the front page of the Dandy was when he gave way to another memorable character - Keyhole Kate. Brought alive by artist Alan Morley to make a popular character of a shy girl who likes to spy on people by peering through keyholes seems strange, but she struck a chord with her readers and remained a mainstay for decades.

If anything the Beano was even more popular than its stable companion. This was also based not just on its ability to create memorable characters, but combined with an inclination towards generally breaking the rules which children could associate with and love. This even before the arrival of Dennis the Menace. Sales soared to over a million copies with regular deliveries being made to forces serving abroad. Clumsy strong girl Pansy Potter was soon established as a firm favourite. Girls loved Minnie the Minx who would stand for no nonsense from bigger boys. Wearing her iconic black and red striped jumper she is constantly in trouble. It is not so much that she goes out to break the rules, it is just that she thinks there shouldn't be any rules to start with.

Lord Snooty is the Eton educated Lord Marmaduke of Bunkerton Castle. In his early strips he makes friends with some local kids whom he invites to live in his castle and so Lord Snooty and pals were born. Snooty's catch phrase was: 'Snooty by name but not by nature'. The success of D.C. Thomson's authors and illustrators continued to be their ability to create characters that appealed to a wide audience. Today these characters would be marketed as 'brands' where fortunes are made by licensing. Who also could imagine stars of radio and films allowing their images to appear in comic strips without their agents demanding huge payments. It was these stars who appeared regularly in Radio Fun and Film Fun, both of which were popular during the 1940s and beyond.

It was the huge popularity of the silver screen that encouraged the launch of the Film Fun comic in 1920. Along with a plethora of film related magazines Film Fun gave the industry an opportunity to influence the younger generation in the hope that they would become regular cinema-goers into adulthood. The comic was published each Tuesday with a cover price of tuppence. It featured Laurel and Hardy who often appeared on the front page. Other firm favourites included Harold Lloyd and Joe E. Brown. The strips were sketchily drawn and increasingly featured war or armed forces related stories. As with other children's comics propaganda was seldom far from the surface.

Although not published until October 1938, Radio Fun became a success as the stars featured could be heard by youngsters on an almost daily basis. It also sold for tuppence and was published each Thursday. Staggered publication of the various titles tempted children to spend their pocket money on more than just one favourite. Radio Fun's early use of colour attracted many readers who were able to follow the escapades of their favourites in strip form. Big hearted Arthur Askey and 'Stinker'

Murdoch being amongst the most popular. Old Mother Riley and Sandy Powell also enjoyed regular coverage. Cockney comedian Tommy Trinder was counter balanced by stories concerning the very posh Western Brothers. Appealing to a children's audience was important for performers and so it was that acts as diverse as Flanagan and Allen, plus of course Tommy Handley were happy to add their names to the long list of entertainers appearing in Radio Fun.

Whilst many initially dismissed the value of comics, in retrospect they did much to raise the morale of youngsters growing up in uniquely difficult times. A bridge between comic strips and more serious books was provided by a number of comics aimed at youngsters entering their teens. The Wizard and the Champion had been providing stories of adventure and derring-do since 1922. They were joined the year before the outbreak of war by Hotspur. Many well known writers, including Dennis Wheatley, contributed stories. There was an emphasis on fair play and bravery. Just like the output of the BBC, youngsters were encouraged to develop into the type of adult the country would be proud of. To modern eyes this may seem strange even misguided, but it was a different world. The fact that we were at war deepened our suspicion of foreigners who always featured as the baddies in these tales relayed by the likes of Hotspur.

In a sense from the moment children started school they were being groomed, not just by their parents and teachers but also by the children's media to produce the type of child who would eventually serve the country and its empire. We were indoctrinated with love of country and the Royal Family. To respect those in authority, teachers, the police, doctors. The list was endless of what and what not to do. It was only the likes of the Beano that gave a glimpse of what was to come. A touch of irreverence and the testing of the status quo.

Chapter 13

It's that Man Again and Again and Again

On Tuesday 15th October 1940 the film 'The Great Dictator' starring Charlie Chaplin had its premiere in New York. Back in London this fact was not included in the news bulletin being read to the nation by announcer Bruce Belfrage. His well modulated voice never wavered or missed a beat as in the background a loud explosion could be heard. Above a bomb had crashed into Broadcasting House. Smashing through the seventh floor it finally came to rest two floors below in the music library killing seven members of BBC staff. Belfrage finished the news bulletin and programmes continued uninterrupted. The upper lip of Britain had never been stiffer. The previous day the King and Queen had visited Neville Chamberlain in hospital. Within three weeks his death was announced on the BBC. Many within government and the corporation wanted programmes during the war to be confined just to news and public announcements, but this was a battle they were never going to win. The public wanted and needed to be entertained.

It is easy to forget that radio was still in its relative infancy, with the BBC having only been formed into a national corporation in 1927. An early decision was made to merge what had previously been a series of regional platforms. The new national station was called the Home Service. However, due to the continued bombing of London various departments were dispersed to safer parts of the country. The wireless had become as important in war-time Britain as television or the internet is today. It soon became obvious that the public were increasingly unhappy with the meagre diet offered by the Home Service. Classical music, recitals, censored news bulletins and seemingly every gap in the schedules filled by Sandy MacPherson playing the theatre organ.

To fill the need for lighter music and entertainment a Forces Network was established but even here our troops at the front were pursued by Sandy and his organ. There was no escape. Luckily there was better to come and soon a mixture of popular music and variety proved so successful that before long a huge percentage listening to the network were civilians. The audiences continued to grow, with dramas and quizzes winning over a new group of listeners. The network was on air for twelve hours a day from eleven in the morning until eleven at night, eventually to be expanded with transmissions starting at 6.30am.

The popularity of the Forces Network is underlined by taking a snapshot of the Home Service schedule in December 1943. Starting at 7.00am the news was followed by music by César Franck. At 7.55am time for 'Lift up your hearts' a religious talk which ran until 1967. Then a five minute news bulletin followed by (you guessed it) theatre organ music performed by Sandy MacPherson. A talk 'Christmas is coming' was followed by the morning service for schools. A military band played until 12.30pm. At this point if anyone was still tuned in there was an edition of Workers' Playtime. This popular show was shared with the forces programme and at least offered some light relief. Broadcast live from factories around the country with the headline act usually being a well known comedian.

Things did not get a great deal better in the afternoon with a mixture of sombre music and programmes for schools until Children's Hour started at five o'clock. The evening entertainment featured music by Brahms and Dvořák. Those seeking popular music were not going to find it here. Instead a concert of music by Haydn. Finally a glimmer of hope for those philistines who did not like classical music, a programme featuring Ivy Benson and her band, but only after a series of serious talks. Then at 11 o'clock a final news bulletin and close down. Doubtless there were loyal Home Service listeners, but it is obvious why the Forces Network captured so much of the available audience. True, the Home Service was informative and educational but actual entertainment remained thin on the ground.

With the radio often being kept on all day in many households children became regular listeners, particularly to comedy programmes. Hearing recordings of these programmes today it is obvious why they appealed to children, because most of them do feel strangely childish and frankly banal often relying on laughs from corny catchphrases. Whilst music endures over generations, spoken comedy has a much shorter sell by date. This becomes obvious listening to recordings of the most popular war-time comedy programme ITMA (It's that man again). It was launched in 1939 and ran for ten years. It stared Tommy Handley, a quick fire comedian from Liverpool. It went through a number of incarnations during its lifetime and featured a number of settings but the format was always similar. ITMA was based on an American show starring George Burns and Gracie Allen. The scriptwriter Ted Kavanagh aimed to tell a new joke every minute to emphasise Tommy Handley's ability with the speed of his patter. The problem was that most of the jokes seem pretty tame now eighty years later. The scripts allowed Handley to surround himself with a cast of bizarre characters who soon became household names in their own right.

As audiences swelled to some twenty million each episode was eagerly anticipated. Simple catchphrases like 'I don't mind if I do' slurred by the drunken Colonel Chinstrap was enough to send seemingly the entire population into uncontrollable fits of laughter. Any mention, no matter how oblique, drew the same response from the old boy and the studio audience. Never missing a chance to have a dig at the enemy the show featured a hopeless German spy called Funf and the Italian Signor So-So. Any joke directed at foreigners, particularly if they had funny accents, was a signal for the audience to burst into long bouts of uncontrollable laughter followed by applause. The greatest reaction was reserved each week for Mrs. Mopp, Handley's daily help. Their banter always culminated in her catchphrase 'Can I do you now sir?' This was as near to suggestive innuendo allowed under 'auntie's' watchful eye. In fairness ITMA was trying to break new ground for British comedy shows and as such is still remembered today.

Whilst comedy shows were becoming ever more popular Sandy MacPherson was not about to be sidelined. Despite the BBC's theatre organ being destroyed in 1941 he then started his own 'Sandy MacPherson's half hour'. Astonishingly at the beginning of the war he was on call for up to twelve hours a day and later he even pursued troops serving as far away as India. There really was no escape.

With the need to lighten the mood of the country other comedy shows were also commanding huge audiences. 'High Gang' was created by the American comedian Ben Lyon along with his wife Bebe Daniels. They had found a format that was well received as they travelled the country and managed to persuade the BBC executives that it would also work as a radio show. They recruited the popular comedian Vic Oliver to join them. Starting in 1940 when the news was grim and everyone needed cheering up. This the show managed to achieve with much of the humour directed at ridiculing Hitler and his cronies. The show's success encouraged stars like Noel Coward and Stanley Holloway to appear as guests. Again High Gang's humour appears very dated now but back then it created a new type of comedy format.

'The Happidrome' started in 1941. It ran for six years rather than just the six shows originally planned. Starring Harry Korris it was broadcast live each week from the Grand Theatre Llandudno. Also featuring Cecil Frederick and Robbie Vincent, it was based on the running of a small provincial theatre. Known as Ramsbottom, Enoch and me, the trio remembered by Shirley Balmer and Roger Fry for the song 'We three in Happidrome working for the BBC'. Variety Bandbox was a firm Sunday night favourite on the BBC and became the launchpad for many future stars including Frankie Howerd and Tony Hancock. As children we all loved these shows which we really thought were funny and entertaining, and it was quite a tonic to hear adults laughing for a change.

Popular music helps form our childhood and teenage years. Each generation becomes nostalgic when they hear songs that dominated their formative years, perhaps even more so during times of war. Of course everyone remembers the songs made popular by Vera Lynn. The lyrics of 'We'll meet again' and 'The white cliffs of Dover' played on the emotions of troops longing to return home. There was disquiet in government circles that felt sentimentality would weaken the resolve of our fighting men. This fear was also being shared by the Nazis, but there was a weird coming together centred on one song loved by the opposing forces.

Originally recorded by the German cabaret singer Lale Anderson in 1941, 'Lili Marlene' was picked up by British soldiers listening to German forces radio. In an astonishing twist the song was recorded by Anderson the following year in English. Why? Stretching credibility further the English lyrics were credited to Norman Baille-Stewart, an English Nazi imprisoned before the war as a spy. Having travelled to Germany he was eventually arrested and was the last British man to be imprisoned in the Tower of London.

By 1943 the arrival of the Americans in Britain witnessed a huge demand for music played on the American forces network which started broadcasting on Independence Day of that year. Soon the young were jiving and jitterbugging to the sounds of Glenn Miller and his Army Air

Force Orchestra. Sandy MacPherson was still banging away on the BBC but increasingly theatre organ music sounded out of step with the times. Who wanted to listen to him when the close harmony and glamour of the Andrews Sisters were on offer.

A source of fascination for youngsters during the war was the strange messages relayed regularly after news bulletins. Few of us realised at the time that these were being sent to secret agents working under cover throughout Europe. Of course most of them were false leads but cushioned somewhere in their midst were genuine messages. Each one was read out very slowly and repeated. For example 'The violin has lost a string. The violin has lost a string.' Few people listening at home had any idea as to the significance (if any) of these messages, but for agents in occupied territory they were a matter of life and death. Sometimes the contact was made via a piece of music played at a particular time and there were reports of radio producers complaining as their planned schedule was interrupted. Even complaints from them that a scratchy record had been played offending their professional pride. No matter, the producers were always over-ruled and firmly rebuked.

One of the best known radio voices during the war belonged to Doctor Charles Hill. His name was not used however, being known simply as 'The Radio Doctor' due to auntie's non advertising policy. He was appointed by the Ministry of Food and began broadcasting his regular five minute slot in 1942. His down to earth approach to all things medical struck a chord with the public. He had the ability to describe the most complex matters in language the public could understand. He was particularly concerned that the country's bowels were open and working well. The sale of prunes, when they could be found, soared.

The sounds of the 1940s still evoke memories in those who were young at the time. A recording of an air raid warning still alarms after all these years, while the music and voices from the war years create a feeling of nostalgia. Those voices made so familiar by the radio add to the pieces of the jigsaw that forged our childhood.

Chapter 14

Book Worms

With no iPads, computer, television or social media, the children of the forties had far less distractions. On a wet afternoon in the summer holidays many turned to books to occupy them. Rather like radio plays, reading allowed youngsters to put their own interpretations on the story being told.

With war restrictions creating a shortage of paper, many explored old favourites that were still in print. Anne Prowse remembers the first serious book she read was 'Swallows and Amazons' by Arthur Ransome. Girls were well served with 'Black Beauty', still as popular as ever sixty years after its first publication. It seems that virtually every girl in the land had read 'Ballet Shoes' by Noel Streatfeild. The book was illustrated by her sister Ruth Gervis who went on to teach art at Sherborne school and subsequently the Sorbonne. Gervis was a relatively minor player in a supreme clutch of book illustrators, including Margaret Tarrant who published her 'Nursery Rhyme' book in 1944. Margaret Mary Tempest illustrated the 'Little Grey Rabbit' books written by Alison Uttley. These were immensely popular with 'Little Grey Rabbit To The Rescue' published in 1945 and she was busy with other projects during the war years.

Illustrations helped bring stories alive and it is Mabel Lucie Attwell who became a household name during this time. Although primarily an artist she did write a series of story books during 1943 and 1944. To be successful in any of the arts your work needs to be instantly recognisable and Attwell certainly ticked all the boxes required. She produced endless variations of tubby, lovable children in countless amusing situations. She was one of the first to realise the potential of marketing. Her images were used in greeting cards, jigsaws and pottery figures. She was also active in advertising a wide range of products. Her success was not lost on one of the period's best known authors. More of Enid Blyton later.

One of the most prolific and successful children's writers was Elinor Brent-Dyer whose 'Chalet School' series eventually ran to sixty four books. Starting back in 1925 the tales were set in a large chalet in the Austrian Alps. Initially the setting provided a beautiful backdrop to gentle stories of schoolgirl life, but the outbreak of war changed all that and Brent-Dyer tales suddenly had a hard edge. In 'Chalet School In Exile' published in 1940 the school has to be evacuated as the pupils and teachers are threatened by Nazi sympathisers and they have to flee. This is reckoned by many to be Brent-Dyer's finest book.

The following year the author confronts the war full on in 'Chalet School At War' with the girls moving on first to Guernsey and then on to the Welsh borders. Two further war-time books followed with 'The Highland Twins At The Chalet School'. By the time 'Gay Lambert At The Chalet School' is released just prior to the end of the war the school has grown in size and fame and its author is back in more typical territory. Brent-Dyer's books during this period are unusual in that she did confront problems, both factual and emotional.

It is doubtful if any boys read the 'Chalet School' series. They wanted more raw excitement and danger from their authors. A template for a fine British hero was set down by 'Bulldog Drummond', a character created by H.C. McNeile. The 'Bulldog' books were referred to by one wag as 'snobbery with violence'. Heroes had to be public school officer class. They are brave, fearless and highly moral. Those from less privileged backgrounds are also good chaps, providing they know their place. All foreigners are dodgy, dishonest crooks and criminals. There is an assumption that Britons are somehow an altogether superior race. This manly invincibility is perpetuated by 'Biggles', written by Captain W.E. Johns.

'Biggles' (James Bigglesworth) was undoubtedly partly based on his creator. Johns had seen active service in the Royal Air Force during the first World War. He finally relinquished his commission in 1931. He actually left with the rank of Flying Officer but once he had started on his writing career he always referred to himself as Captain W.E. Johns. A strange decision although apparently allowed as he had commanded an aircraft. These social niceties were obviously important to him and may give a clue to the character of 'Biggles'.

Johns was a prolific author completing over one hundred and fifty books over a long career. His first 'Biggles' book was published in 1932. The main character and those of his chums were very much in line with the perception of a typical British hero. Fearless, good hearted and a thoroughly good egg. During the war years twelve 'Biggles' stories were released, although one of them 'Biggles Secret Agent' related to events before the war which meant that its successor 'Biggles In The Baltic' was the first story to be set in a war-time background. War brought an extra potency to his tales and sales soared as youngsters waited impatiently for their hero's next escape or triumph. Warming to his task Johns had 'Biggles' popping up all round the different theatres of war, from the South Seas to the Orient.

In 'Biggles Defies The Swastika' he gets caught in Norway by the rapid German advance. Never fear, he passes himself off as a German sympathiser even becoming an officer in the Luftwaffe before escaping on a motorcycle to Sweden. Nothing seemed to stop this gung-ho super hero who makes James Bond look like a beginner, until finally in 1943 his luck appears to run out in 'Biggles Fails To Return', but as ever he survives to the delight of thousands of young boys who remain hooked on his adventures. In a time when youngsters needed to enjoy the thrill of danger, albeit second hand, Captain Johns supplied it in spades and still has a sizeable following today.

W.E. Johns, Elinor Brent-Dyer and Enid Blyton were all born within a few years of each other in late Victorian Britain. A time when the map of the world was splurged in red indicating the massive reach of the British Empire. All their work reflects this in that they viewed Britain as a positive force in the world and so projected their characters in a light that many find worrying today. Most fire is directed at Enid Blyton, presumably because of her colossal popularity although many other children's authors at that time preached a similar sermon which they honestly thought was based on firm moral ground. Today much of this is deemed xenophobic, sexist and racist, but if it was this went over the heads of most children reading the yarns at the time. Everyone I interviewed for this book remembers reading and enjoying books written by Enid Blyton.

She remains even today one of the most commercially successful writers of all time with worldwide sales in excess of sixty million. As with most aspects of her life her extraordinary output has been questioned, having completed over seven hundred books in addition to endless articles for magazines. Is it really possible for an author to churn out fifty books in a year? Suspicions have been raised as to whether she employed ghost writers, a claim she strongly refuted and certainly no-one has come forward to suggest differently.

Even her method of writing caused raised eyebrows. Apparently she would sit in front of her typewriter with no set plan or draft. She insisted that the story just unfolded without any prior thought or planning. Other writers have claimed a similar reaction as if the copy was being guided by some outside force, but none to the extent of Blyton. Of course all authors write to a background of what is happening in their own private life. After the birth of her two daughters, Gillian and Imogen, Enid's marriage ran into trouble. Her husband, probably feeling excluded due to his wife's astonishing work load, began to drink heavily. It appears he was jealous of a close relationship that Enid struck up with the nurse who had been brought in to help with the birth of Imogen. True or not her husband, Hugh Alexander Pollock, walked out and was never seen by his children again. Some years later she married the surgeon Keith Durrell. Despite living in idyllic surroundings her daughters viewed their mother very differently. When young the girls were supervised by their nanny as Enid powered away on her typewriter. Gillian, the older daughter by four years, remembers her mother with affection but Imogen is less forgiving. As with so many successful parents the children whilst loved often suffer under a spotlight that is seldom allowed to fall on them. Success as with failure always comes at a price.

Like Mabel Lucie Attwell, Enid Blyton was very commercially aware. She was one of the first authors to offer some of her characters for licensing. This obviously accelerated later in her career with the appearance of Noddy and Big Ears. The very volume of her output and the range of subjects she covered opened up many opportunities. They ranged from adventure, mysteries and stories featuring animals to numerous short stories on the life of Jesus. The 1940s was one of her most productive periods.

Perhaps in response to the 'Chalet School' books Blyton produced her own 'Naughtiest Girl In The School' series. These were followed by six books covering life at 'St. Claire's School'. The very volume of her output tends to obscure the overwhelming success of a series of books seemingly remembered by almost all who were growing up during the war. The 'Famous Five' tells of the adventures of Julian, Dick, Anne and Georgie. Perhaps it was due to the fact that children at that time tended to go around in close knit gangs, but there was definitely something about these youngsters that struck a chord with a whole generation. In 1944 the first in the adventure series was published. Increasingly Blyton was turning to seaside locations for her inspiration and the 'Island Of Adventure' was the first in a series of eight which rivalled the 'Famous Five' in popularity. Again the main characters of Dinah, Lucy, Ann and Jack had a familiar ring. Her books were thought by critics to be just a variation on a theme. Cardboard characters they may have been, but thousands of children associated themselves with one or other of the youngsters on the printed page. The criticism of Blyton's books were mirrored by ever increasing sales. Who was having the last laugh?

Whilst it is true that you can't tell a book by its cover, illustrators have always been central to success in children's publishing. Enid Blyton used a variety of artists to illustrate her massive output, but perhaps it was Eileen Soper who was the most influential. She was responsible for over fifty of Blyton's tales, but importantly it was she who captured the essence of the 'Famous Five' helping to bring alive the group of friends who apparently enthralled an entire generation. Soper was also an author and a prolific illustrator of a wide range of children's books, including 'Polly Piglet' and the 'Teddy Bear's Party'. Eight years younger than Blyton, it could well be that her own popularity restricted her association with the best selling author. Like so many of her contemporaries, Soper was a very interesting character. She studied under her father, the painter George Soper who illustrated amongst others 'The Water Babies' and 'Alice In Wonderland'. Something of a child prodigy Eileen had already exhibited at the Royal Academy by the age of fifteen. She was a great lover of nature and gardens and with her sister maintained her father's garden in Hertfordshire as a nature sanctuary. A woman ahead of her time and just one of an impressive collection of women illustrators who have yet to receive their full recognition.

One of the most welcome presents in a bulging stocking on Christmas Day was an annual. These books featuring favourite illustrated characters were supplemented by stories and puzzles. Some of the most popular featured characters from the 'Beano' and the 'Dandy'. Another comic strip character who appeared in the Daily Express was amongst the most sought after. 'Rupert Bear' was the creation of Mary Tourtel and was launched in 1920. It no doubt helped that Mary's husband was the editor of the Express. It was he who wrote the captions until his death in 1931. Mary's eyesight caused her to pass the mantle for 'Rupert' to Alfred Bestall, an artist who had illustrated the 'Blighty' magazine during the Great War. At first Bestall closely copied Tourtel's style, but over the years he gradually refined the leading characters and his stories became rather more realistic. He continued with the strip until his retirement in 1965, although he was called on to illustrate the 'Rupert Bear' annual until 1973. Rupert with his red jumper and yellow trousers is fondly remembered by children over several decades. They enjoyed his adventures with his friends, Bill Badger, Edward Trunk and Algy Pug. One notable lover of this enigmatic cartoon was Paul McCartney who bought the rights to 'Rupert Bear' shortly after the Beatles broke up.

Whilst boys were really well catered for with a variety of Christmas annuals available, the market for girls remained rather poorly served with only 'Blackies' annual for girls which been available since the 1920s.

Alongside films the wireless, board games and sport reading in whatever form helped youngsters enjoy some escapism from a dull drab and sometimes dangerous world. The written word opened up a world of imagination, but also helped form so many of the interests that they carried over into their adult lives.

Chapter 15

Got any Gum Chum?

There was a popular song that was even being played on the BBC. It ran to many verses, but there was one that stuck in the mind and was particularly important for the whole of the country:

> 'Over there, over there
> send the word, send the word over there
> that the Yanks are coming,
> the Yanks are coming
> the drums are rum-tumming everywhere'

The area around the American Embassy in Grosvenor Square was already known as 'little America' with around two thousand staff bolstered by numbers of military personnel. Britain was about to be swamped by a huge influx of U.S troops shipped across the Atlantic in purpose built Liberty ships. Luxury liners were also requisitioned including the Queen Mary and Queen Elizabeth. There was not a great deal of luxury on show for the thousands squeezed aboard. Prompted by the surprise attack on Pearl Harbor in December 1941, the Americans now entered the war in earnest.

From the beginning of 1942 the Yanks really were coming with the first troops arriving in Belfast on 27th January. Within a year over two hundred and fifty thousand had been transported to Belfast, Glasgow, Liverpool and Bristol before being deployed. They were followed by even greater numbers. It was time to meet our new trans-Atlantic cousins. It is true to say that this was not an instantaneous love match. There were suspicions on both sides.

The Americans were issued with guide books warning of touchy areas that were likely to cause offence. There were to be no wise cracks about the Royal Family or the food and warm beer. For many young recruits it was the first time they had left their home town or state. Arriving in this grey depressing country must have been strange, the locals were odd too. Wary, suspicious and yet the GIs had come to save them (or so they thought). Despite sharing the same language, words often had different meanings. A side walk was a pavement, a picture house was a cinema. The innocent secretary seconded to work for the Americans soon realised that asking for a rubber rather than an eraser could really land them in hot water. Very soon British resentment led to the Yanks famously being referred to as 'over paid, over sexed and over here'.

It was the British kids who saw through the problems the adults were constantly moaning about. To most children and certainly their older sisters the Yanks were a gust of fresh air. For a start they looked better. Taller, smarter, they were almost to a man friendly and outward going. It helped that their uniforms were made of soft material rather than the coarseness of the uniforms worn by British squaddies.

In fact the Americans were so smart that they looked like an army of officers. The pay differential between the Allied Forces was an instant cause for resentment with the U.S soldiers being paid up to three times more than the Brits. The Americans filled the best restaurants and pubs, grabbed the best looking girls and left our boys feeling like the poor relations. All of this made little impression on the young. They loved the Yanks who always seemed to have pockets full of sweets or chewing gum to hand out. In Kettering troops driving in a Jeep would regularly throw oranges to children standing in the street. What was wrong with the grown-ups, the Yanks were great.

A mass observation poll confirmed that the Americans were less popular than the Dutch, the Czechs and Poles. Even the free French had a higher rating with Russians being the most admired. To underline this the red flag fluttered proudly over Selfridges in Oxford Street. Tensions filtered their way right to the top of the military command. The Americans could not understand the officer class attitude to the men serving under them. They thought the British class system corrosive. This was most apparent in the exclusive cavalry regiments described by an American officer as 'the most mentally inert, unprofessional and reactionary group in the British army'. How, they wondered, could any self respecting soldier serve such snobbish idiots. But of course they did as they had done for centuries. The British counter to this claim related partly to race. They were horrified that the black troops were segregated in a form of military apartheid which continued until 1948. There was also a feeling in British high command that slack discipline within the U.S troops would come home to roost on the battlefield. Two systems with much misunderstanding set against a dangerous and implacable foe. Initially it did not bode well but perhaps it was the children that helped to unravel this dilemma. They are instinctive, reacting naturally to people and events before they are influenced by the prejudices of adults.

In London the democracy of the American forces was not so noticeable in their accommodation arrangements. Officers had already taken possession of the former premises of the National Sporting Club in Piccadilly. In 1943 the government requisitioned the Great Room at the Grosvenor House Hotel on Park Lane as the mess for American officers. The non-commissioned ranks were not forgotten with the formation of the Rainbow Club on the corner of Denman Street and Shaftesbury Avenue. Here was a slice of America right in the heart of London. There was a choice of restaurants and cafes serving food not available in Britain. The building was not only a draw for thousands of U.S troops, but also waves of young British women looking for a good time as well as spivs selling black-market goods. Actually the club itself was not seedy and tried to create an atmosphere to make GIs feel, albeit fleetingly, at home. As well as good food the club hosted dances and cabaret featuring well known stars. A twelve year old Petula Clark was cheered to the rafters when she starred at the club in 1944.

Like most children Jean Sporle loved the friendly American soldiers except the white helmeted 'snowdrops'. These were members of the United States Military Police Corps. They carried long batons and she noticed that everyone seemed to give them a wide berth. At the slightest sign of trouble they would wade in. They were a regular sight patrolling the streets of the West End, usually walking in pairs. Soho was something of a haven for deserters, but all feared the stony-faced military policemen. There would be no gum or sweets from these guys.

Whilst Jean's mother was at work she had a babysitter to look after her. It did not take long for the young girl to invite her boyfriend round. He was an American soldier with the unusual name of Angel. He would arrive with bags of candy for the eight year old Jean. She was puzzled why on most occasions the couple would leave her and go upstairs on the understanding that she would not tell her mum in return for more sweets

No talking in class.

The author, always happiest away from school.

Arthur Price-Jones pictured on the right with his twin brother Vernon.

Ronnie Pitt with his adopted family and RAF airman Newton Palmer.

A Wellington bomber and crew at RAF Husbands Bosworth.

Martin van Oppen and his brother - ready to take on the 'vaccies'.

Not a nit to be seen.

Bomb sites were regularly used as adventure playgrounds.

The rag and bone man was a regular site on the streets of Britain.

Derek McCulloch, known as
Uncle Mac, fondly remembered
by a whole generation.

The Beano. Comics were central to many youngsters' lives.

Enid Blyton's books were criticised by adults but generally devoured enthusiastically by the young.

The Americans were generally popular with children as they always seemed to have pockets full of sweets.

The 'buzz bombs' brought fear and destruction, particularly the V2 which devastated whole areas.

Celebrations in London on VE Day.

A 'V' for Victory formation during the Victory Parade.

Anne Prowse, who spent the war in India and Burma.

Sheila van de Velde, a young teenager pictured just before her return to Britain from South Africa.

Charlie Weber, part of an eternal triangle brought on by his absence fighting in the war.

Rose Sheran pictured with baby Tony who only found out about his true father as a teenager.

Phil di Meglio, who never forgot Rose and was reunited with his son just prior to his death.

1947 snowfall crippled the whole country for weeks.

A unique view of a snow covered Buckingham Palace taken from St. James Park.

A poster advertising the 1948 'austerity' Olympic Games.

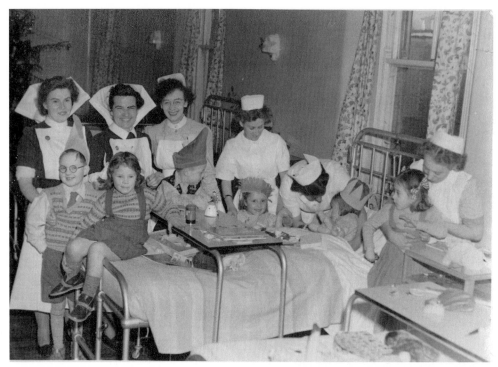

An early NHS children's ward, all smiles and starched uniforms.

Sergeant Peter Twiddy, killed in Albania in 1943 and finally buried with full military honours on what would have been his one hundredth birthday.

A young Lesley Taylor. Me and my teddy bear. 'Got no worries, got no cares'.

Jean Sporle, having survived the war enjoying a paddle with her mum.

The author with his sister Ann on holiday at Cayton Bay near Scarborough.

Sergeant Gerry Southworth, an early conscript to National Service.

and presents. Angel eventually left to take part in the Normandy landings. He survived and what's more came back and married the babysitter, taking her back to the States. That is where the happy story ends. Like many young English girls she thought she was heading for a life of luxury. All they knew of the States they gleaned at the cinema. Everyone appeared wealthy, the reality came as a horrible shock. Living in a trailer park was no fun. Her husband, who had appeared so glamorous and attractive in uniform, reverted to being a lazy, uncouth, hard-drinking bully. Within two years she was back in Hammersmith. Marriage was not encouraged by the U.S military but there was a steady stream of GI brides who set off for a new life in the States. It's always difficult to settle in and to be welcomed in a totally new environment and marriages floundered, but those who persevered often found genuine happiness whilst still keeping in touch with family and friends at home.

In his diary Evelyn Waugh bemoaned the fact that fashionable central London had been invaded by hordes of American soldiers and young women, and even those old enough to be their mothers hanging around waiting to be picked up. Warming to his theme he recorded: 'there swarmed out of the slums and across the bridges multitudes of drab ill-favoured adolescent girls and their aunts and mothers never before seen in the squares of Mayfair and Belgravia. They passionately and publicly embraced in the blackout and at high noon and were rewarded with chewing gum, razor blades and other trade goods.' Snobbery was still alive and well in Britain.

It is doubtful if grumpy old Evelyn Waugh would have approved of Iris Chapple's mother or her friends. They would regularly go for a drink at the Dorset Arms on Clapham Road in Brixton. The mums would leave their children outside and within minutes an American service-man would appear with lemonade. Sweets would follow and if they were really lucky a packet of Smiths crisps with the famous blue twist of paper containing the salt. Iris loved everything about these service-men, their accents and particularly their easy-going manner. Unlike British adults these young men did not talk down to the kids. Eventually often hours later her mother would reappear red faced and giggly, but brandishing the ultimate prize - a pair of nylons. Iris never criticised her mum as they were desperately poor and she surely deserved some light relief from a life of drudgery, albeit drudgery very close to the centre of power. Her mother set off each day before daybreak to clean at 11 Downing Street, the home of Kingsley Wood the Chancellor of the Exchequer.

Some ninety miles from London young Ronnie Pitt was still living in Sibbertoft in the heart of the English countryside. Only ninety miles in distance but a million in reality. Living as he was with a religious family brought young Ronnie Pitt into contact with the first black men he had ever met. They were stationed at the nearby airfield and one of them came to lunch at the house on a Sunday after attending chapel. He was Leading Aircraftman Newton Palmer who was from Jamaica and he sometimes preached at the chapel. No doubt he found the services rather dull compared with those he was used to in his home country. He was gentle and charming. It is interesting that there appeared to be no colour prejudice in the area which he found astonishing compared to back home. It was only after the war with greater numbers of West Indians arriving in Britain that trouble started. For the moment most British people in both town and country showed little or no animosity.

Back in London Iris and Jean became aware of a change of mood. The war had swung in the Allies' favour. The streets were thronged with a heady brew of different uniforms. Added to the Tommies and Yanks were the Canadians who hated to be thought American because British folk found it difficult to differentiate the accents. The free French strutted whilst the brave Polish airmen were applauded. Particular favourites were the Aussies with their distinctive slouch hats. It was almost as if people could sense victory in the air.

Rather than an instant love affair generally the Brits and the Americans had gradually come to terms with each other. These seemingly brash young men had travelled halfway across the world to help us. Grudgingly most came to admire their outgoing approach to life. Certainly the young were converted, leaving the old to mumble into their cups of tea and warm beer. For their part the Americans realised that once their initial reserve was broken down the British could be warm in their own way and prove to be good friends. Certainly many old pals continued to make annual trips to Britain after the war. Then just as there appeared to be a real understanding they were gone. In the south of England endless convoys of trucks and tanks trundled towards the coast. In London restaurant owners stood at the door anxiously looking for customers who no longer appeared. The theatres and cinemas were half empty and the street-girls even contemplated getting an office job or working in a factory. Britain longed for peace but suddenly life was drab again. There was still rationing, power cuts and a cold winter ahead. Still victory of sorts finally seemed assured. Or was it?

Chapter 16

We Thought It Was All Over

A week before all the roads to the coast had been clogged. Huge transporters bearing heavy artillery pieces, tanks, personnel carriers and jeeps. The soldiers waved to those lining the streets. They waved, gave the thumbs-up and the 'V' for victory sign as children shouted encouragement and waved Union Jacks. Later many of those cheerful young men lay dead on the beaches of Normandy.

The 6th June had seen the beaches stormed and breached despite heavy losses and the Allies were now entrenched in France. The tide of war had turned and despite the long road ahead the news was generally good. Then exactly one week later Hitler launched Vergeltungswaffen, the reprisal or vengeance weapon. On 13th June a strange black flying object was seen travelling towards London. It was surrounded by a rather ominous red glare and it gave off a sound rather like a car in low gear. Suddenly civilians were to find themselves back in the front line again. Was this Hitler's last throw of the dice? If so it was a frightening one.

The V1 rocket was an un-manned missile powered by pulse-jet, programmed so that when the fuel ran out it dived to earth. The ten rockets launched on that first day met with mixed success. Designed to bring terror to London half of them failed to make it across the Channel. Those that did reach their target gave an indication of what was to come. Despite only six people being killed in Bow the rockets caused massive damage in the neighbourhood. At home there was a news blackout as the politicians and military high command tried to assess this new threat. The first sustained attack took place on 15th and 16th June with over two hundred and fifty missiles being launched with over seventy reaching the heart of London. Still no official news, the population were being treated as if they were all idiots. The British government continued to retreat into secrecy, whilst all around people were being killed and homes ruined.

On 18th June one hundred and twenty one worshippers were killed when a rocket fell on the Guards' Chapel in Birdcage Walk as they rose to sing the 'Te deum'. No respecter of class or age, this new monster descending without warning from the sky was in danger of causing panic. The slogan of 'keep calm and carry on' was needed as never before. After just three days of attacks some five hundred people had been killed and the violent blasts had devastated a swathe of homes, warehouses and factories. Many thought the buzz bombs, or doodlebugs as they were known, were more frightening than the Blitz because of the haphazard nature of the rockets. Londoners wandered about staring up at the sky ready to dive for cover once the engine above them cut out. Up to one hundred and fifty missiles a day were now being launched. It was calculated that if this rate of carnage continued within a couple of months the effect would be greater than that endured during the length of the Blitz. Something had to be done. Now it was not only London that was suffering. By mid September Kent had been subject to over two thousand rockets while Sussex had endured close on one thousand. Luckily a fair proportion of these fell on open farm land but were frightening none the less.

Back in Brixton trouble continued to haunt the Chapple family. Iris and her mother had already been bombed out twice in the Blitz but Hitler appeared to have a very personal grudge that was still to be played out. Because her mother was deaf young Iris now had the added responsibility of listening out for any buzz bombs flying nearby. Luckily she was able to warn her mother as the V1 plunged towards them. There was a blinding flash, a deafening screech and seemingly all around them crumpled and crashed. Dust as if from a desert storm clogged their nostrils. The sudden silence was eerie. Blinking through a haze Iris can remember seeing her clothes hanging on the washing line seemingly untouched by all the mayhem surrounding them. Unharmed they extricated themselves from the wreckage. Lady luck was still on their side.

Public morale was suffering. The rockets were spooky with that frightening pause between the engine cutting out and the carnage to follow. Strangely the V1s created only a very small crater when they landed but their blast power was far greater than conventional bombs which was demonstrated when a rocket fell on a house in our road killing the occupants. Neighbouring houses appeared undamaged yet further up the road our windows were blown out. Luckily I had been sleeping right next to the window and was untouched by the flying glass.

On 30th June after a wet and miserable summer the sun came out at last. In the centre of London young women paraded in bright summer frocks and men took off their jackets and removed their ties. Ruining this carefree moment came the familiar sound of a doodlebug. Looking skywards people dashed for cover as the engine cut out and the rocket dived towards the packed street. Aldwych shook like a wounded animal and the dust and debris totally obscured the summer sun. As the air cleared it was possible to see lines of burnt out buses appearing like ghosts from a horror movie. But this was real. Sprawled across the road and pavements lay the dead and injured. Forty two dead and hundreds injured as the wailing sirens of ambulances and police cars struggled to get through to give help. A nurse attending the scene reckoned that no battle scene could have been any worse.

London's railway stations were once again crowded with youngsters being evacuated for the second time. It has been rumoured that double-agents were feeding false information about the damage being done by the missiles. Rather than hitting a trophy target like Tower Bridge the majority were falling short, smashing into the suburban areas of south London. Anti-aircraft guns were not aimed at the incoming rockets as the damage done by shooting them down would be just the same as if they were allowed on their way and so for the time being the V1s arrived unchallenged. Eventually on 21st June the decision was taken to transport all the anti-aircraft guns out of London and set them up on the North Downs giving them an unrestricted field of fire. Banks of barrage balloons were deployed and fighter squadrons instructed to hunt the flying bombs down before they could reach the capital. These actions, although largely successful, came too late for the seventeen hundred people killed in the first two weeks of the V1 attacks. In addition thousands had been badly injured with widespread damage and demolition of houses.

The V1s were being launched from sites in France but they were increasingly being neutralised by the advance of the Allies. Seemingly the threat had passed. With the false confidence that seems to be the preserve of prominent politicians, Duncan Sandys, the prime minister's son-in-law and Minister of Supply confidently announced that the threat from flying bombs was over. His announcement to the press was followed within twenty four hours by the arrival of the V2, which was larger faster and far more deadly than its predecessor. Measuring almost fifty feet in length and carrying a ton of explosives, whilst travelling faster than the speed of sound, these monsters plunged Britain into a feeling of despair. Every time an end to the war seemed in sight another body blow was landed by the Nazis. A wet summer was merging into a cold miserable autumn. Was there going to be no end to the suffering?

Launched from mobile platforms the V2 travelled too fast for it to be heard. Enter the silent killer, a weapon so lethal as to cause widespread alarm and foreboding. The first V2 rocket fell on Chiswick. The noise of the explosion was unprecedented. Rumours suggested that it was the result of a gasometer blowing up. The loud double bang could be heard miles away. Once again the government kept details of the new threat from the public, but they did institute a new total blackout. The speed of the missiles meant there was no warning and no time to find shelter. Still stupidly the government attributed the increasing carnage to plane crashes and unidentified explosions. The public were not buying it. Despite thirty six rockets hitting London in September, followed by over one hundred and thirty in October it was 10th November before Churchill advised parliament that 'for the past few weeks the enemy has been using their new weapon -a long range rocket against us'. As probably almost three hundred V2s had already landed on London by the end of November surely the public had already worked that out for themselves.

Within two weeks of the Prime Minister finally coming clean about the V2 rockets there was an horrendous attack on the Woolworths store in New Cross. This was particularly distressing with many children among the one hundred and sixty dead. A contemporary report referred to 'things were falling out of the sky, bits of things and bits of people.' A young girl was quoted as saying 'a horse's head was lying in the gutter. There was a pram hood all twisted and bent and there was a baby's hand still in its woollen sleeve.' Where Woolworths had been there was nothing, just an enormous gap covered by clouds of dust. No building, just piles of rubble and bricks and underneath it all people screaming.

Until the Aldwych disaster the West End had got off relatively lightly. It couldn't last. Within a month a further forty five people were killed in an attack on fashionable Kensington. Then it was back to south London again as Marks and Spencers in Lewisham was hit. Once again bodies were strewn around like rag dolls. It was reported that the stress caused some who had narrowly escaped to hold their hands to their heads they screamed hysterically. The war had become totally dehumanised. Nerves had been stretched to breaking point.

It is these first hand accounts that emphasise the horror that Londoners were still having to endure. Although the news of the Allied advance was encouraging it failed to lift the sour public mood. There were now more industrial strikes than there had been in peacetime, the weather was foul and freezing and still the bombs kept coming. On 8th March Smithfield retail market was packed with housewives picking up their scant meat ration. Without warning a V2 rocket crashed into the heart of the market. Panic and pandemonium. Many workers were trapped in the cold store. They were lucky as they were eventually rescued, frozen but safe. Robin Burns's father was working for the heavy lifting service unit. He said it was a scene from hell. So dreadful that it was difficult to distinguish the carcasses of the cattle and sheep from those of humans. Eventually the death toll rose to one hundred and ten with many more seriously injured.

Everyone who survived the buzz bomb attacks have their own tale to tell. My father was in a street close to Aldwych when the V1 rocket fell causing such a catastrophic loss of life. A cab pulled up and my dad joined the driver under the vehicle. They emerged shaken but unhurt. Earlier eight year old Jean Sporle was pulled to the floor by her mother. There was a frightening explosion. Staggering to their feet they hugged each other. As the dust gradually cleared they realised how lucky they had been. All the windows were shattered and twisted masonry hung from the ceiling. Jean's mum had just about been to serve their meagre roast. Undeterred they set the table which was now minus a leg and had to be propped up with books. Solemnly they sat down to eat. Peering through a gap in the wall their neighbours were surely impressed to find them not only safe but eating their Sunday lunch despite it being covered in dust. Surely a supreme case of 'waste not, want not'.

With the arrival of Spring weather came better news of Allied victories. Surely now the end was in sight, despite the continued shortages with even potatoes disappearing from many shops and the bacon ration being cut. Evacuated children were welcomed home again. Those, that is, that still had a home. Millions had been destroyed or badly damaged. Britain was like a boxer who had taken a terrible beating but was still standing. A winner on points perhaps, but the effect of the fight would have huge and lasting implications for years to come.

Ivy Millichamp was a housewife in her thirties. Living in her tidy bungalow just outside Orpington she was no doubt looking to a brighter future now the end of the war was drawing ever closer. In a macabre form of April fool's joke she became the last civilian to die on British soil during the war when a random rocket struck her home. Within a month it was time for the country to celebrate and party.

Chapter 17

Days to Remember

The unemotional voice of BBC announcer Stuart Hibbert had stated that tomorrow would be Victory in Europe Day and Prime Minister Winston Churchill would address the nation at three o'clock. Meanwhile in Potters Bar a seventeen year old Pat Desbruslais, who was in her final year at boarding school rushed to the school chapel. Pushing open the heavy door she clambered up into the bell loft. For the first time in five years the bells rang out in celebration.

I was woken by an ear-splitting scream. Thinking something dreadful had happened I rushed downstairs. I was engulfed in hugs and kisses from my mother and neighbours who had gathered to drink a bottle of Haig whisky that my father had saved from before the outbreak of war. From amongst the excited conversations I gathered that at last it was over. As a seven year old I understood that life for all of us was about to change, but it was still all very confusing.

Do omens really exist or do they mostly just turn out to be coincidences? There were two strange meteorological events in London indicating both the beginning and the ending of the war. In the early morning of 3rd September 1939 a storm described as being of Wagnerian intensity broke. As the thunder rumbled ominously and lightning flashed it was as if the gods were angry and giving a warning of what was to come. Over five years later in the early morning of 8th May 1945 another storm developed over the capital. Again rain lashed down, thunder crackled and lightning danced across the rooftops. This time it was as if the storm was clearing the air. Cleansing by washing away, albeit temporarily, the burden of war.

Over in Hammersmith Jean Sporle's parents had decided to 'go up west' to join in the festivities. Carrying a little Union Jack attached to a stick, it was obvious to the young girl that the whole mood had changed. Normally a journey on the tube was to be confronted with rows of miserable faces avoiding eye contact. Today everyone cheerfully joined in conversations despite sitting in sodden clothes. Nothing, not even the British weather, was going to ruin this day. By the time the train arrived at Trafalgar Square station they had to fight their way through crowds to get onto the platform. Outside it had finally stopped raining. Jean had brought a bag of scraps to feed the pigeons. It was still only about eleven o'clock and crowds stood around seemingly not really knowing where it was best to be. Some were heading off down the Mall towards Buckingham Palace, but Jean's dad thought it was too early as the Royals wouldn't appear until the afternoon. Instead they rather aimlessly headed past the National Gallery and up the Haymarket towards Piccadilly Circus.

There were flags and bunting hanging from office buildings and many young women were sporting red, white and blue ribbons in their hair. The crowds were swelling and the mood was infectious, helped by bottles of drink being offered around. From humble brown ale to Krug champagne it was as if a hidden brewery had been discovered. It was obvious that many people would be drunk by lunchtime but the mood was still boisterous and friendly. By the time they had jostled their way to Piccadilly Circus the noise levels had risen to a pitch of overall excitement. Jean and her mum joined in a line dancing the Conga. People were singing some of the old Cockney songs as everyone joined in a rousing rendition of the Lambeth Walk.

The statue of Eros had been boarded up. An officer from the Tank Corps was the first to clamber up followed by a paratrooper who hauled up a pretty young blonde to a chorus of wolf whistles. There were uniforms representing all branches of the armed forces together with dozens of Americans in uniforms. Polish airmen were hoisted onto the shoulders of the crowd. Two GIs joined the growing group on the boarding protecting Eros to huge cheers. The mood was mad as if all the tension of the conflict had been released. Microphones had been rigged up all around and at three o'clock the crowd finally quietened as there were short speeches from the King followed by the Prime Minister. With a voice quite filled with emotion he said 'We may allow ourselves a brief period of rejoicing but let us not forget for a moment the toil and effort that lie ahead.' The crowd cheered but the toil could wait, for now it was all about celebration. Churchill concluded 'Advance Britannia, long live the cause of freedom, God save the King.' The cheering swelled but Jean noticed other people crying, remembering perhaps friends or family that had not survived or those still fighting in the far east. Looked at in retrospect Churchill's words appear rather hollow. Britannia was about to retreat rather than advance on the world stage, but that was for another day. For now it was a time to throw off British inhibitions to drink, dance, sing and rejoice.

Jean and her parents joined a tide that pushed them back down again to Trafalgar Square. On they went under Admiralty Arch and on down the Mall. It was estimated that there were over one hundred thousand revellers in the West End that day. Squashed in amongst a crowd of adults that were towering above her, Jean suddenly heard a swell of cheering and a very tall American hoisted her onto his shoulders. She could just make out the King and Queen along with the young princesses on the balcony, accompanied by a fat, bald headed man, Winston Churchill. How the crowd cheered but Jean reckoned that half the crowd were tipsy and they were willing to cheer almost anything that moved. No matter, she had witnessed an historic day. She was asleep by the time they reached Hammersmith station and her father carried her home and soon she was tucked up in bed.

All across the country there were similar celebrations, albeit on a smaller scale. In Oxford a huge bonfire was started at St. Giles the Martyr's Memorial. There was an outpouring of happiness and relief tinged with sadness, particularly in towns and cities that had suffered from severe bombing. In Belfast huge crowds gathered. Some danced the Conga in front of immobilised trams. In Kingston upon Hull Queen Victoria Square was filled with dancing revellers, as were Pickering Park and Queen's Gardens. Liverpool was not going to miss out and across the city excited crowds gathered to a background of chiming church bells. The opening hours in the pubs were extended for an extra hour and impromptu street parties were set up with tables lining the streets with excited children eating their way through mountains of jam sandwiches. Over the coming weeks street parties were arranged across the country and remain a vivid memory for many of freshly baked cakes, sandwiches and jellies.

In Glasgow, Southampton, Birmingham and of course Coventry, D-Day was celebrated to the full against a background of bomb sites. Shattered buildings relieved for a moment by bunting draped across the scarred spaces in a vain effort to deflect from the devastation caused by the Nazi bombs. In market towns and villages church bells also rang out. The following day was also to be a public holiday. A day to fight off hangovers and sober up. A day also to reflect and each one to think of the challenges that lay ahead. What did occur over the following two months changed the lives of every man, woman and child.

Perhaps the doomsters were wrong. Rationing and shortages were annoying, but the weeks passed and the public mood brightened. Christmas was celebrated albeit on a reduced scale. On New Year's Eve toasts were made for the first time without blackout curtains. A new future beckoned. Was it really going to be as dire as many had predicted? For most children war offered an exciting background as they failed mostly to understand the magnitude of events taking place. Many were evacuated, experiencing a life in the country totally alien to them. Some were lucky and enjoyed the experience, but many became unhappy and made to feel unwanted. However children have a great ability to adjust to whatever is thrown at them so they were undaunted as they charged enthusiastically into the new year.

Previously, a general election in July produced a stunning landslide victory for Labour. Churchill, the great war leader, was trounced. Even in his own constituency, despite Labour and the Liberals not contesting the seat, a local farmer captured twenty five percent of the vote. Although not really understanding the implications I remember feeling sorry for this old man who had been at the centre of our resistance in the darkest early days of the war. To the voters he now seemed out of touch in a country that demanded change.

In August 1945 the Americans dropped an atomic bomb of terrifying power on the Japanese city of Hiroshima. From that moment the world was changed forever. War had always been brutal from the days of clubs and spears but atomic power had produced a weapon that totally dehumanised conflict. Even during the dogfights taking place over our skies, there had been at least a token nod to the days of chivalry. The buzz bombs had acted as a warning and now the Allies could only thank God that they had acquired the ability before the Germans had a chance to further devastate Britain and the rest of Europe. Savage and ruthless as it was, the bomb certainly shortened the war in the far east and saved thousands of Allied deaths and casualties.

The euphoria of victory did not last long. Those who had mistakenly hoped for a rapid improvement in their lives were disappointed. It gradually sank in that the war had all but bankrupted the country. Shortages and rationing persisted. As the year tottered to its end disillusion set in. Even Christmas was dull and miserable for many.

Seven year olds and younger children could remember nothing but war. They had listened to adults wistfully discussing life before the hostilities started describing a time of plenty, with no rationing, plentiful food and well heated houses. To the young it sounded almost too good to be true and for them unfortunately it was. This did not stop them dreaming of better times to come. Children had endured much over the past five years. Bombs, absent fathers, rationing and that all encompassing cold in winter. Surely life for everyone was going to be better.

Part II

Same Old Austerity

Chapter 18

Homecoming

Five years earlier Sheila van de Velde had set sail for South Africa with her family. They had survived a heavy bombardment in Liverpool the night before their departure and then their ship had been pursued by German fighters, but now they were back, and what a day for them to dock in Tilbury. Their Union Castle Line ship had been kept waiting off shore to allow troop ships to be discharged and that night they heard that the following day was to be celebrated as Victory in Europe Day, the very day of their arrival.

It was with a mixture of excitement and some apprehension that Sheila peered through the mist and rain as they approached the shore. She had left Britain as a child but was returning as an attractive young woman of seventeen. Five years is a very long time in a youngster's life and living abroad in some style was in sharp contrast to what she was expecting on her return home. She was going to miss the colour and vibrancy of Africa, as well as the good food and the wonderful climate. Her father had returned to England over a year earlier to take up a senior position at the head office of the Marconi Organisation. For that period Sheila, her mother and three siblings were living in a waterfront hotel in Cape Town waiting for a berth. Having left school she took a job as a secretary but also spent time helping to look after the injured in a military hospital. Eventually a cabin did become available allowing them to enjoy a crowded but uneventful voyage home.

As they approached the shore they noticed billowing smoke coming from bonfires that had been lit in celebration. There was a distant sound of church bells, whilst on the dockside hundreds of uniformed troops milled around. Flags and bunting had appeared on all the buildings. After clearing Customs they were driven away through streets where tables were being laid out for street parties, groaning with stacks of food. Not the spread that Sheila had become used to in South Africa. No creamy ice creams or exotic fruits, just mountains of jam sandwiches and hastily baked cakes. Sheila's father had bought a substantial detached house with a large garden in the Essex village of Ingatestone, so the young woman continued to live in comfort compared to most living in post war England. Servants and relative luxury were to be relics of the past but the challenges ahead were exciting. With the fine weather of that late summer Sheila shocked the locals by the brightness of her African clothes and the briefness of her shorts as sun tanned she cycled through the sleepy village. The tan gradually disappeared but never the memories of Africa.

On that same May day in 1945 whilst Sheila arrived back in Britain, her future husband was working on a forestry camp in Bodfari, north Wales. A week earlier he had cycled down with three school friends from Wakefield. Walking up a muddy track they saw a tractor careering at high speed towards them. Sliding to a halt an excited German prisoner of war told them that the war was over. The irony was not lost on them to be informed by a man who until moments before would have been their enemy. Anxious not to miss the celebrations at home they set off on their long ride back to Wakefield. There they joined in street parties that carried on quite oblivious of the rain that continued to pour down. The flags and bunting looked bedraggled, hanging limply from the town hall although it was lit up at night. It was still a novelty not to be stumbling round in the dark, hopefully a sign pointing to a better future.

Whilst Sheila van de Velde had enjoyed a privileged upbringing during the war years, the super rich and well connected sent their children to the United States. The platforms of London train stations were filled with a cast of blue-bloods sobbing and waving their children goodbye, often for the duration of the war. Who could blame them? Many had family connections living in country estates or New York mansions. Much of the popular press was critical but for some of the aristocracy it was time to cash in some favours. 'Chips' Channon was besotted by his son Paul. For 'Chips' it was more of a sacrifice to be parted from him than letting him take his chance dodging bombs in London. Young Paul had to slum it with the Astors and other mega wealthy connections before returning home. There remained in Britain just a few thousand families that owned vast tracts of land and retained extraordinary wealth and power despite the huge rise in taxation. Their connections stretched like tentacles worldwide. Wherever 'Chips' travelled he could be sure of an influential welcome and doors being opened for him. The children of this coterie returned to Britain after the war expecting their life of privilege to continue, but life and attitudes were changing. Eton and the Guards still beckoned, but increasingly this set was going to have to rely on clever accountants and tax advisors to maintain their social dominance. Many succeeded, but others saw their country estates either demolished or sold off to people who had made fortunes during the war. The industrialists and nouveau-riche were now invading the grouse moors, Ascot and even some of London's establishment gentlemen's clubs.

The end of the war had not brought much in the way of cheer. If anything life for most was worse with increased rationing and restricted electricity supplies leading to frequent power cuts. The mood was increasingly tetchy and grumpy. What had all the sacrifices made really achieved? Millions of service personnel were still waiting to be demobbed, but on 8th June 1946 London finally hosted a gigantic victory parade. If the country was looking for a morale boost the weather certainly did not help. The day dawned damp and drizzly. The doomsters predicted the celebration was too little, too late. It would be a damp squib just like the weather. They were wrong. In places the crowds were twenty to thirty deep. Leaving on the first tube train of the morning I went with my mother and sister up to central London. We found a space at the top end of Whitehall near Trafalgar Square. Union Jacks and flags of the Allies hung from public buildings and offices. Ranks of uniformed servicemen lined the route as I peered between them, having been pushed to the front of the crowd. We could hear military bands playing as first in the parade were a group of top brass saluting languidly as they passed. The parade stretched to four miles including some five hundred military vehicles representing all branches of the armed forces but led by the Royal Navy, the senior service. There were tanks, mounted ack-ack guns and massive missile-like bombs carried on groaning trailers plus amphibious landing gear. The civilian organisations were not forgotten. An ARP heavy lifting unit was represented as were ambulances and a gleaming fire engine. With excitement growing and the noise of military bands representing of all the Allied Forces, each proudly bearing their national flags. Now a swell of cheering as waves of troops from across the continents marched by with the precision that must have taken endless rehearsals to perfect. Fierce looking turbaned Sikhs, Africans smart in their pressed khaki and the much feared Gurkas, all were wildly cheered and the volume went even higher as to the skirl of pipes and the swirling of kilts the Scottish contingent marched by.

Still they came, the Aussies to louder cheers still. Then tough looking Canadians, Kiwis and South Africans, each trying to out-do those preceding them. Then came the Yanks to wolf whistles, all swagger but less regimented and seemingly more relaxed. Unfortunately the Cold War was already under way denying the Poles their place in the parade despite the heroics of their pilots in the skies above Britain. None either from any of the countries now forming the USSR.

The spectacle continued to be breathtaking, particularly for the children watching in awe. The sound of marching feet to a background of military bands remained long in the memory. Eventually the Royal Family appeared in the state Landau to emotional applause and cheering. And then it was all over, but not for long. We joined a long human tide heading down The Mall towards Buckingham Palace. Eventually the doors to the balcony opened and the Royals waved to a crowd that stretched as far as the eye could see. It is strange but at these moments the country appears to come together. The feeling never lasts long as different agendas are set and division takes hold again. As youngsters this never concerned us, generally being eternal optimists by nature. The diarist 'Chips' Channon assured Emerald Cunard 'How quickly London had recovered from the war and how quickly normal life had resumed'. Maybe for him and his cosseted clique but for the majority life continued to be a constant struggle.

There were real problems with servicemen returning to civilian life. That is those who had been demobbed for there were still many thousands awaiting their release, some still trapped abroad. When the men finally arrived home there was often trouble that broke out within days. The longing to get home was often so intense that the reality became a massive disappointment. Many who had served throughout the war had become institutionalised. They had ceased to think for themselves. Arriving home they found their jobs had either been taken by women or even worse by someone who had avoided military service. Men who had achieved rank in the forces were often obliged to serve under someone whom they despised. There was resentment and rancour. At home life for many was also unsatisfactory. Many a romance heightened in times of war had cooled and soured. Jealousy reared its head. Had either been unfaithful? Who knows, who cares after all these years but it did cause doubts and rifts. But in a time when divorce was only available to the wealthy most couples soldiered on. For others there were some very nasty surprises awaiting them upon their return home in the form of a baby or a child that their wife or sweetheart had kept secret from them.

It was often children (even those fathered by the returning servicemen) that caused the most trouble. Children who had not seen their father for years became unduly attached to their mothers. They resented this strange man who had invaded their house. It took time for the new regime to settle in. Suddenly behaviour which had been fine with their mother was questioned by the new arrival. Many men were particularly worried about their sons. They had been molly-coddled and needed to be toughened up. So it was that all these tensions surfaced although in time an accommodation was normally found and family life resumed. Of course there were many wives and children who were thrilled to welcome their husband or dad back, but the whole country was having to learn how to adjust to a new life and a new Britain.

A close friend of my father had been captured by the Japanese during the fall of Singapore in 1942. He spent the rest of the war in Japanese POW camps and working on 'the railway of death'. Returning home I remember a man with hollowed out eyes and the body of a scarecrow. Bent and racked by malaria he gradually fought his way back to health. He was Jewish, rather countering the claim of many that generally the Jews avoided military service.

Some serving in the war thrived but others it crushed. Martin van Oppen's memory of his father before being posted to the Far East was of a quiet but confident man. The man who arrived home was a stranger. It was as if his experiences had drained him. He was a husk of his former self. This decline was to play heavily on their family life and on his parents' marriage. And so it was that the tentacles of war spread and affected us all. The British tendency to bottle up their emotions did not help. Many who were children at the time told of their fathers never even discussing their time in the war. There were tales of screams and shouts waking them as their dad experienced dreadful nightmares, but still no explanation, no purging of the soul, just silent suffering.

The partition of India saw another influx of home-comers as the last of the Raj returned. One of these was a young ten year old girl who was about to arrive in her mother country for the first time. What a shock to come from a life of servants and privilege to the cold dormitory of an English boarding school.

The early years of Anne Prowse's life were spent in Digboi in Upper Assam bordering Tibet. Anne's father was the company doctor for Burma Oil. The Assam refinery was the oldest in Asia. It was a division of the Burma Oil Company. By 1943 the threat of a Japanese invasion sent the family moving south to Ootacamund known as 'Snooty Ooty' and not without reason. Founded as a resort by the British it sat amongst the mountains of western Tamil state. Here was one of the strongest upholders of the Raj and the social life revolved around the extremely Snooty Ooty club. As a doctor Anne's father's status allowed the family to mix in influential circles.

Anne was packed off to boarding school at St Hilda's in the town before ending her Indian education in Darjeeling. The family lived in a typical large colonial bungalow complete with an impressive veranda. They had a large staff including a butler, houseboys, cleaners, gardeners and several cooks whose kitchen was reached through a covered walkway. Anne was very close to her ayah who shared her mosquito net but slept on the floor at the foot of her bed. Looking back Anne is horrified by the way the staff were treated with so little respect. The sense of the supposed in built superiority of the expats had almost run its course in India, but for the moment it continued to thrive. Strangely this does not appear to have been the case in Africa. At least in Sheila van de Velde's case where she remembers their Zulu servants being much admired and treated with consideration.

It was probably the growing violence and discontent in India that led to Anne being sent to England to further her education. In 1946 she set sail for Britain accompanied by a friend of their family, a Mrs. Crossfield and her daughter Yoma. They travelled on a cargo ship departing from Calcutta. They were held up for days in the Suez Canal as military vessels still had precedence. What a shock it was to dock in Glasgow on a snowy February morning. All grey bleakness. How Anne was going to miss the searing sun, the dazzling colours and even the smells of India.

After a seemingly endless train journey they arrived in London. Then onwards to stay with relations in Kent before joining the school chosen for the two young girls. Effingham House was a small private boarding school in Little Common near Cooden Beach in Sussex. The school only had sixty three pupils and Anne was designated that number making it sound more like a prison, but she was happy enough there. Holidays were spent with the Crossfields or with relatives. At weekends the girls were allowed to cycle into nearby Bexhill. When travelling to visit her grandparents in Thornbury she was met in London by a 'universal aunt', women who were designated to ensure safe passage for unaccompanied young girls. Anne had to wait another year before partition prompted her parents to return to England.

Those early post war years saw a mass return of Brits all affected in one way or another by the war. Without doubt most would have been truly disappointed. Cities pockmarked with bomb damaged buildings. People generally moaning about the ongoing austerity which was still being ratcheted up with increased rationing, shortages and power cuts. Was this really what victory should feel like? So much anticipation met by a wall of anticlimax. For everyone the consequences continued to rattle around.

For some returning there was an unexpected bundle awaiting them. Yet another hurdle to confront. Wounded pride and a feeling of being humiliated. Was it time to walk away or to swallow your pride?

Chapter 19

Surprise Packages

With some four million troops being demobbed between 1945 and 1947 it was no surprise that there was a surge in the birth rate. A few years earlier there had been growing concern about the number of illegitimate births. Letters and articles in the press bemoaned falling moral standards. Much criticism came from the ruling class including politicians conveniently forgetting their own frequent lapses. Reading the diaries of 'Chips' Channon gives an insight to their golden world where bed hopping appears to have been a regular feature of their lives and wasn't confined to the opposite sex either. As the Cole Porter song said 'Anything goes' providing of course there is no public scandal.

For the average middle class or working class girl the risk of pregnancy and the shame caused hung heavily over them. But war brings an added temptation. The instant attraction magnified by the chance that the couple would soon be separated or that one of them could be killed added a certain frisson. Many a few minutes of passion was followed by circumstances that blighted a girl's life for years. Whilst hurried marriages often turned sour when the serviceman eventually returned home.

The problem became even more acute with the arrival of American troops in Britain in 1942. Over one million US troops were stationed in Britain in the two years leading up to the D-Day landings. Just under ten percent of the servicemen were black, an added cause for concern for the British government. They were perplexed by the Yanks' insistence on segregating their armed forces. They were wary of endorsing this policy as the British had millions of black and brown troops from the empire fighting for the mother country. Herbert Morrison, a Labour politician and minister, tried to step carefully around the problem. A memo marked 'secret, must be kept under lock and key'. It stressed that worries about the outrage this segregation policy would cause in Britain. What really exercised the Home Secretary was the possibility of British girls mixing with black GIs. He mused 'That the procreation of half caste children would create a difficult social problem.' He further advised 'To avoid the birth of such children the government was keen to discourage the mixing of black troops and local women, proposing that white women should not associate with coloured men. It follows that 'they should not walk out, dance or drink with them'. There was little hope of this suggestion being followed. Many British women found these softly spoken and polite Americans charming.

The black troops were initially rather taken aback by their relatively warm welcome in Britain. Many came from the southern States where they were still treated harshly and denied many rights. Britons' attitude to blacks and Asians was often formed by the teaching at school. Britain portrayed itself as an influence for good, bringing the advantage of their expertise to the local population. Britain wanted to be seen as benefactors helping people that they viewed almost like children. The reality generally was at best extremely patronising. No matter, for a time the black troops were generally well received. Government advice jars with us now. We were to be 'sympathetic' rather than caring and certainly not to have any social contact other than perhaps at church. After all we were all supposed to worship the same God.

Disregarding colour differences the American military took a very tough stance regarding pregnancies of local women and GIs. A serviceman could find himself transferred overnight and without warning if a birth seemed likely. They then protected their man by denying the girl access to his whereabouts. If the couple eloped and got married the GI was subjected to a court martial. Permission to get married had to be obtained from the commanding officer and this was often denied.

It is estimated that about twenty thousand illegitimate births could be attributed to white American troops in Britain during the war. The numbers fathered by black troops varies, but is reckoned to be in the region of one to two thousand. The attraction of the Americans proved irresistible to many British women of all ages as many of the children born were to married women. There were obviously relatively few British men available with so many serving abroad. The Yanks were so different, easy going, attractive in their smart uniforms and with money to spend. This caused great resentment with the British troops still stationed in the UK. It was difficult to compete and frequent brawls broke out particularly in the larger cities. Further trouble erupted when white men from the southern States took exception to black servicemen escorting white girls. Mass observation noticed a change in British attitudes towards black servicemen when they were seen out in cinemas and at dances. Suddenly these women were being abused and referred to as whores or worse. The British tendency to be wary of anyone different from themselves re-established itself. For some of the young women involved it was all very confusing and painful.

There are many harrowing tales of those black children left behind. For the most part they were packed off to be brought up in local council homes. A lucky few were adopted or kept by their natural mother or grandparents. Others were fostered. Whatever their circumstances it was impossible for the children not to feel like outsiders, aliens almost. With so few children of mixed race living in Britain at the time they were constantly being pointed or stared at. Worse, at school they had to endure taunting and name calling. They needed a thick skin trying to ignore being called nigger or gollywog. Even those that made friends were often rebuffed by the white child's parents when taken home to play. Gradually over the years attitudes changed. Slowly maybe but change was on the way and it is to their credit that so many of these children made such a success of their lives.

For those pregnant mothers left in the lurch aided by the military authorities, it proved almost impossible for them to track down the fathers. The US authorities' view was that it was their duty to protect their own and that enquiries into the father's whereabouts was an intrusion on his privacy.

Being left with a baby out of wedlock was very difficult for the young woman. Fingers were pointed and tongues wagged and yet it was often the innocent girls who fell pregnant. The real good time girls knew how to look after themselves. Some continued to be abused within their own family unit with constant references to their disgusting behaviour that had brought shame on the family. Britain could be a really sanctimonious place to live. The effect on these children could also be profound particularly during their early school years. Being called a little bastard and seeing their mother shunned, initially had hurt turning to rage as the years passed. Time is a great healer and gradually the stigma receded.

Of course life was even more difficult for girls who gave birth to black babies. The tolerance shown initially to the black troops was generally short lived. Many girls were packed off to relatives with cover stories of their daughters working away from home, returning once the child had been born and taken in by the local council. Denied their babies they were sworn to secrecy, ensuring that the scandal never surfaced locally.

Monica, a child brought up by her grandmother, had a very happy and loving home life but outside it was a different story. She never got used to conversation stopping when she walked in a shop and people staring at her. She felt tainted, she said years later, an outcast. Children don't see colour differences until they are influenced by their parents or other adults. Monica had a very good white friend at school who invited her to her home for tea. Her friend's mother on answering the door let out a shriek and shut the door in Monica's face. The friend was then forbidden to play with her. Luckily her grandmother was made of sterner stuff and the child was encouraged to stand tall and be proud of herself which she did, going on to enjoy a successful life. Most children who grew up in council homes did not even know their father's name making it almost impossible to track them down. That is until DNA testing became available, leading to discoveries which were usually too late to reunite the child and their father. A constant theme running through so many stories of illegitimate children is a deep rooted wish to track down their parents and gain a sense of closure.

Like many Tony Weber was too young to remember his father returning from the war. Charlie had been serving with the Desert Rats in north Africa in a campaign that he survived intact. Later while he was still serving with the Eighth Army in Italy he was injured in a bizarre series of events. Whilst on sentry duty Charlie Weber's mate panicked and attempted to run away and he was picked off by a sniper. Staying for a second watch Charlie was also shot several times probably by the same sniper. Bleeding and partially paralysed he was rescued and transferred to a hospital ship where an emergency operation was performed. Months later Charlie was shipped home and sent to Stoke Mandeville hospital. There he underwent extensive treatment which enabled him to regain movement in his right side, allowing him to walk although often in excruciating pain. His wounds never healed and remained with him until his death. Surely he deserved a homecoming fit for a hero, but life is seldom that simple.

After such dreadful experiences it was no wonder that Tony's father could seem remote. Always correct and encouraging but not as affectionate or outwardly loving as towards Tony's younger brother who arrived a year after his father's return. Subsequently three daughters arrived to swell what was generally a happy family unit. Apart from his father's rather cool attitude towards him another worry niggled away. The girls and his younger brother were all slim and fair haired whilst Tony was stocky with a swarthy complexion.

Tony had already entered his teens when one hot night unable to sleep he got up to get a glass of water. Pausing for a moment on the landing he could make out voices below. He could hear his mother talking to her sister. Creeping closer he realised they were talking about him. Feeling rather guilty but intrigued he continued to eavesdrop. The conversation was confusing. Who was this Phil they kept on mentioning? Emboldened and with his ear to the door the talk was now of Glastonbury. He knew his mother had worked there in the war as part of a unit known as the Timber Corps. Then the bombshell. It appeared that his mother had fallen for this American GI called Phil. Shocked, the young boy retreated to his bedroom. It was all very confusing, but obviously his brave stoic dad Charlie was not his father at all. Nothing was mentioned at the time but from that moment Tony's admiration for his dad grew. To come home and find your childhood sweetheart had given birth to another man's child must have been devastating. Many men would have walked away and yet his parents somehow managed to put it all behind them and go on to have a fulfilling marriage and bring up a large and united family. Despite this it set up in Tony's mind a deep rooted desire to find his biological father.

It was a couple of years later that Tony interrupted a rare huge row between his parents. Alarmed, he pleaded with his dad to calm down. 'Dad! Dad!' 'Who are you calling Dad?', Charlie responded. Obviously it wasn't only his war wounds that remained raw and painful. As with all family rows, there were tears and banging of doors. In typical British fashion nothing was said the next day. Instead, rather awkwardly, Charlie offered his stepson his first cigarette. This was a peace offering. A Woodbine and a squeeze of the arm. Mutual love and respect restored. For them, the subject was closed. It was never discussed again. Tony obviously quizzed his mum, but for the moment she refused any discussion. Gradually, over the years, she weakened slightly and with the help of other family members Tony was able to slowly reconstruct his parents' story.

For some, love triumphs despite massive setbacks and heartbreak. First love has an intensity that is seldom forgotten, even in old age. Charlie Weber was eighteen at the outbreak of war. Born in Lambeth, his family, along with many from the East End and others from deprived areas of London, were housed by the London County Council on the Watling estate in Burnt Oak. A few years earlier, Burnt Oak had been a small, rural hamlet just off the Edgware Road (the ancient Watling Street). Thousands of homes were built and a tube station enabled residents to commute to work in central London. There was also plenty of employment to be had locally with factories, including Rawplug, Duples and the de Havilland aircraft factory nearby. The estate attracted many left-wing activists and for a time the area was known as 'Little Moscow.'

Charlie had already been called up for military service by the time he met Rose Sheran. Her family had moved to Burnt Oak from St. Pancras. She was a petite, lively brunette two years his junior. He tried to pick her up in their local pub, but she wasn't playing, not yet anyway. He insisted on walking her home and by dropping his service cap under a bush in her parents' front garden, gave himself the excuse to return. She relented and they started going out together. They were a good looking couple. He was a tall, slim young man who was rather shy and reserved, but a perfect foil for the chatty bundle of energy that was Rose. For the weeks before Charlie was posted they were inseparable. They went dancing and like most youngsters loved going to the pictures at the Gaumont in Burnt Oak and the Essoldo in Colindale. They became engaged just before Charlie was posted to join the Eighth Army, serving first in Egypt and Libya. For a couple of years they kept in touch by letter. Eventually he stopped writing and Rose assumed he had tired of her or had fallen for some exotic girl in a far off land.

As the war progressed, Rose decided that she really didn't fancy working in a factory. She managed to join the Women's Land Army, being assigned to the Timber Corps. She was surrounded mostly by girls who had grown up in the country, so she was something of a curiosity, this little London sparrow. Her unit was billeted just outside Glastonbury in Somerset. During their six week training they were given lectures on tree recognition and the uses for different types of timber in the war effort. They were sent out with experienced staff and were taught how to fell trees and to plant saplings, as well as undertaking nursery work. The workload was physically tiring and the days long. They started early in the morning and, with only a short lunch break, they carried on to 5.30p.m. in the summer or until dusk during winter months. At night there was little to do except listen to the wireless or play cards. All this changed with the arrival of the Americans in 1943, who were stationed in nearby Street. British and New Zealand troops had been stationed nearby previously and there had been a few romances, but the GIs were in a different league. To start with, they had money and were happy to spend it. Dances were organised at US camps. There was live music and gifts of stockings and food that the girls had not tasted for years. They were different, these Yanks. Outgoing, generous and so self-confident. The girls (at least some of them) were caught up in the excitement of it all. It was at one of the dances that Rose met chubby-faced Private First Class Phil di Meglio. Was it unconsciously an attraction of opposites? Not of Rose and Phil, but the difference between Charlie, her first love, and Phil was extreme. Phil was a fast talking, wise guy, always the centre of attention, the exact opposite of the gentle, thoughtful Charlie. Phil was ten years older than Rose and perhaps it was a confidence that maturity brings that swept her off her feet. She was bowled over by his sense of fun and zest for life. They met as often as they could and once again Rose fell in love. Not for her the idea that there is only one person in life you can fall in love with. Whilst there maybe hundreds of people you could fall in love with, there would be millions where no romantic feelings would ever surface. Love was a lottery. War-time, with all its dangers and the prospect of parting, heightened the emotions. British reserve was cast aside and instincts rather than convention held sway.

The tide of war in Europe was changing. 6th June 1944 saw the D-Day Landings in Normandy. For weeks the roads in the south of England had been clogged with military hardware. There was little chance of a lingering farewell as Phil's unit joined the exodus of allied troops across the Channel. The couple never met again. On 25th October 1944 Rose gave birth to a little boy christened Anthony Charles. It was to be almost half a century before Philip di Meglio was to learn that he had fathered a son. He maintained that he had tried to contact Rose, but she had moved away from Glastonbury and her home in Burnt Oak had been destroyed by a V rocket. So life moved on, but he didn't forget her.

When Charlie Weber finally arrived home after the war, thinner than ever and full of shrapnel, he immediately set about finding Rose. It must have been a terrible shock to learn she had given birth to a baby boy. Male pride can be destructive. At first he felt hurt and let down. Circumstances had changed, but Rose remained as attractive and challenging to him as ever. It was time for him to swallow his pride and follow his instinct. He hated Rose having snide remarks being made about her behind her back. He decided he would bring the child up as if he was his own. In the summer of 1946 Charlie and Rose were married in Hendon. For the next forty-seven years the couple enjoyed a good and companionable marriage, successfully bringing up their large family. Tony looked back on his childhood with affection, but the need to trace his natural father seldom left him.

Philip di Meglio was discharged from the US Army on 1st November 1945 in Belgium. Later he sailed from Le Havre to New York, eventually arriving on the Wheaton Victory on 15th May 1946. He then rejoined the di Meglio clan who lived in Chester, Pennsylvania. The family were involved in a variety of businesses, based mainly around the catering industry. The fast-talking Phil branched out on his own, opening Phil's Autos, tapping into the Americans' love of their cars and the open road. He married Helen, a girl of Polish descent, and they had a son, Philip di Meglio junior.

By contacting US Army Veterans Associations, Tony was able to compile a list of di Meglios who had served in the war. He had no idea how extensive it would be. There were over two dozen Philip di Meglios listed. He wrote the following to each of them:

Dear Messrs. di Meglio,
I am writing to you in the belief that you may know the Philip di Meglio who served in the U.S.A. Army in Wiltshire, England during 1944.

The substance of this enquiry stems from a reunion commemorating the war years here in England recently. Philip's name cropped up and there are people here who would like to know if he is alive and well and how he has fared over the years.

I realise, of course, that this is an exercise in nostalgia stretching over nearly fifty years, but I would appreciate any light that you may be able to shed on this matter.

Looking forward to hearing from you.

Yours sincerely,

Tony Weber. P.S.

He was originally known to come from Pennsylvania.

Within weeks he received a reply from a Philip di Meglio living in Chester, Pennslylvania. A photograph taken in service uniform was also enclosed together with a telephone number. With his heart thumping, Tony dialled the number. A rather frail voice answered the phone. Having established it was Philip di Meglio speaking, Tony came straight to the point. He asked 'Did you know a Rose Sheran back in England during the war?' There was a long pause. After what seemed an age the voice, quieter still, now said 'Rose Sheran.' He sounded wistful, obviously casting his mind back. 'Rose Sheran.' There was another long pause. 'Rose Sheran, I sure did.' There was a woman's voice in the background demanding to know what was going on. Tony took a deep breath. 'Phil, my name is Tony, I'm your son.' There was a sharp intake of breath, a strangled cry, 'Oh my God, my God.' Now the phone was grabbed from the old man and an angry voice demanded to know who the hell was upsetting her husband? Then his father was back on the line. He was crying. It was impossible to tell if they were tears of joy or anger.

Tony could only imagine the impact on the di Meglios of this unexpected bombshell. More composed now, the old man kept repeating 'My God, it's my son.' It can't be easy for a wife of almost fifty years to learn her husband had fathered a long lost love child. Diplomatically, Tony told them he would ring back the next day.

That afternoon an excited Phil di Meglio took on a new lease of life as he danced round his small garden. Even Helen, his wife, calmed down. After all, it had happened a long time ago and if the news made Phil so happy, who was she to spoil everything.

There were several more phone calls and plans were made for the two families to meet in Chester. The bookings were confirmed, although Rose decided to stay at home with her husband. She did, however, get to speak to Phil on the phone. No-one listened in on the call, but it must have been overwhelmingly heartrending.

Some months later, ringing to finalise the arrangements for their planned visit, Tony didn't get the response he expected. Phil di Meglio whispered 'You are too late, I'm dying, I've only been given a week to live.' It was obvious the old man was extremely distressed, each breath was rattling across the airwaves.

Although their flight was re-scheduled, it was two weeks before the Webers arrived in Chester. There was a strained silence in the hire car as they made their way down the main street and past the eighteenth century courthouse. They were shocked by the run-down nature of the neighbourhood as they approached Phil's small house. Now the moment had come to meet his father, Tony held back. The knowledge and planning of this meeting had taken years and now he felt an irrational fear that it would all turn sour. They were met at the door by Helen and at once Tony was struck by the obvious physical likeness to his own mother. With a dry mouth and a thumping heart he was shown into a small bedroom. The meeting of father and son combined pain and joy. They fell into a fumbled embrace. Nothing was said, but tears flowed. The old man grasped his son with a strength that belied his appearance. No longer portly, Philip di Meglio had been reduced to skin and bone by the cancer that was killing him. His own son, Philip junior, looked on and the following day Tony was introduced to other members of the di Meglio family who had gathered in curiosity to see this man claiming to be their relative. He certainly had the di Meglio looks. He had a sturdy physique, darkish complexion and was starting to lose his hair. They liked his easy going, informal manner, which was not how they imagined Englishmen to be. OK, he talked funny but they would forgive him that. They formed a huddle in the corner of the crowded bedroom, whilst the English guy held Phil's hand. Eventually, they declared with a theatrical flourish 'OK, this boy is a di Meglio, welcome to the family, Tony.' Then, formally, each in turn embraced him.

Tony spent several days at his father's bedside. Phil was becoming progressively weaker and not much was said. His father moved in and out of consciousness, but always holding onto his son's hand with a firm grip as if this alone was his passport to life. With the timing that only a film director could get away with, Philip's body was being carried out to a funeral car as Tony arrived on the last day of his visit to say his final farewell. It was as if the desperately ill man had hung onto life just long enough to meet his son and now he was going home it was time to take his leave. He died aged seventy-eight and the date was June 1992.

Here was just one of thousands of love stories thrown up by the war gently moving to its conclusion. Three people, two of whom had never met each other, yet remained linked together. It was as if their lives had been choreographed so that they all left the stage in quick succession. Rose died in February 1993 to be followed by Charlie shortly afterwards. Ordinary people have extraordinary lives, which are magnified in times of war. True love never dies but it can be impossibly complicated.

Chapter 20

Relative Values

We can all choose our friends but we are stuck with our families. Mine could easily have been drawn from central casting. Unfortunately Ealing rather than Hollywood. Many could have been seamlessly incorporated into the comedy films being produced by the studio during the 1940s.

Our family tensions arose from religion and perceived differences in class. Of all the players my parents were certainly not the most colourful, but their romance and marriage can act as a starting point. Church Street running just off the Edgware Road in central London, a market street alive with small shops, market stalls and traders shouting their wares. Each morning residents were woken early by the noise of the barrow boys racing to get the best pitch. My mother's father ran a number of local bakeries in the area. The family lived above their main outlet at the grander end of the street close to Lisson Grove. On the same side of the road but down towards the rougher end near Edgware Road my father's mother eked a living selling lengths of elastic and other small haberdashery items. This end of the street was demolished by enemy bombs during the war.

My parents' wedding took place in the rather posh surroundings of St. James's Catholic church in Spanish Place. No father ever thinks the man his daughter wants to marry is good enough and the bond between my mother and her father appears to have been particularly strong. No doubt he wanted the best for his rather beautiful girl and neither Jack Hutton nor his family really measured up. When he died just before the wedding he left a number of properties and what was in those days a fair amount of money.

My grandmother (maiden name Mary O'Brien) married Frederick Hutton aged twenty one in 1887. Her new surname blurred her Irish roots but there was a strong anti-Irish prejudice in London at the time. One that I feel was shared by my mother's family. Worse, Fred Hutton, described variously as a plumber's mate, labourer or jobbing carpenter, appeared to have been unemployed for long periods. Enter the matriarch, his wife Mary. Standing under five feet in height she ruled her large family even into old age with the meerest lift of an eyebrow. How she managed on selling lengths of ribbon and the odd ball of wool remains a mystery. Much to Fred's horror his wife signed the pledge and continued to rail against the evils of alcohol to anyone who would listen. Fred was forced to seek out funerals to attend in order to sink a few pints in honour of the deceased. It was rumoured that he hovered outside churches where funerals were being held in the hope he could infiltrate the wake afterwards.

As a youngster I can remember that granny Hutton would drive my mother to distraction sitting in the corner of the room tutting her disapproval of seemingly everything as she waited to be served her next meal. Drinking, swearing and the way the young dressed all met with her muttered complaints. But was she all she appeared to be? The 1901 census finds Mary and Fred living at 48 Queen Street Marylebone. By this time they have four children including my father who is just five months old. Also listed is John O'Brien, described as a brother-in-law. This is a false entry as he is listed as being twenty six years of age whereas he was actually only sixteen in 1901. The suspicion is that John was actually my grandmother's son born out of wedlock. It seems likely that Fred took on this young girl and her baby. Mary was just nineteen at the time. They married two years later and John was brought up within the family unit.

Difficult as my grandmother might have been she was a remarkable woman. Apart from Fred junior who was killed in the Great War, all her children became successful. My uncle Tom became a town clerk, smooth uncle Arthur a stockbroker and aunt Kathleen (Kitty) married a pompous director of Jays the London department store. My father, having left school at fourteen, attended evening classes at the Regent Park Polytechnic, eventually becoming a senior local government official. I remember being taken by a uniformed attendant up to his office in County Hall, which was as long as a cricket pitch overlooking the Houses of Parliament.

It must have taken great resolve and character for a woman to have virtually single handedly guided her children to a far better life than she had experienced. Having erred as a young woman she was determined her children would prosper. Tiny in size, but steely and single minded, she succeeded.

Unfortunately like so many mothers of her generation she suffered the loss of a son to the Great War. Luckily the circumstances of Fred's death were kept from her. I was told by one of his brothers that having survived a long stint at the front he spent the first night of his leave in a local brothel. Like most of his mates this was probably their first chance to have sex as the opportunity prior to marriage was so restricted at the time. What a shame that his introduction with a young French girl was to be his last. It is likely that flushed with the excitement of it all he drank far too much. Along with his friends they made their way back to camp on foot, no doubt singing as they went. It was a cold frosty night making walking difficult along rutted roads. With several miles still to be unsteadily negotiated they managed to get a lift on the back of a horse-drawn cart, getting them back just in time not to be put on a charge. Hours later they gathered sleepily for a roll-call. It was only then that it was realised that Fred was missing. Surely he had not gone AWOL. A search was organised and poor uncle Fred was found dead in a roadside ditch having died of exposure, although not the kind his mother would have been proud of. Instead she was informed he had died on active service, which in a sense he had. For my grandmother her boy had died for his country and certainly nobody ever suggested otherwise to her.

Why had I as a ten year old child always been so keen to visit my other grandmother who lived in Harrow each week during the summer holidays? It involved a half hour journey on a 142 bus and a single stop on the district line. True I did mow her lawn on each visit but it was the slug of whisky she added to my morning coffee that really appealed. It was a conspiracy we shared and never divulged to my mother. It was this rather rebellious side to my grandmother's character that struck a chord. In a time when conventional behaviour was generally upheld (at least in public) her attitude I found quite liberating, although it would be thought of as irresponsible by most today.

On my visits to Harrow I would often browse through a photograph album whilst she was having her afternoon nap. Generations of forgotten relatives and friends peered out in sepia that somehow added to their appeal. Shots taken in West End studios or in front of porticoed houses.

Many dated back to the Edwardian era, the men looking restrained in their suits and stiff collars. The clothes worn by the women were far more flattering, all wide brimmed hats and long skirts. Among this sea of the unidentified were two figures who stood out. My grandfather had more than a touch of Ronald Coleman about him with film star good looks, but it was shots of my grandmother when she was young that captivated me. She was gorgeous. Maybe she was flattered by the fashion of the day but to a young boy she was perfect. There was one particular shot that stuck in the mind. Possibly a photograph taken on the day of their engagement. They were seated opposite each other captured in profile gazing into each other's eyes. It sounds corny but so romantic. I was about to enter my teens when on a subsequent visit I noticed the album was no longer wedged into the bookcase. I was horrified when my grandmother informed me that she had thrown it into the dustbin as she thought it to be of no interest to anyone. She may have looked romantic when she was young but age had hardened her. I never forgave her. She had no soul.

For a couple of weeks during our summer holidays my sister and I accompanied by our grandmother were packed off to the seaside town of Broadstairs. We stayed at a house owned by aunt Lou and her husband Monty. Also living in the house was aunt Hilda, like Lou a sister of my grandmother. Aunt Lou had spent her early years as a chorus girl with a troupe controlled by C.B. Cochran. Aunt Lou must have been very pretty as a young woman, now she was vague, feminine and slightly dotty but warm and affectionate. Neither of the aunts had ever had children and appeared to be on a mission to fatten me up despite the rationing restrictions. I have memories of plates piled high and every mouthful being watched by these well meaning old ladies.

Their attention was rather overpowering and so given the chance I went out to seek the company of the exotic and eccentric Monty. He fascinated me. A sturdy but rather stooped figure, his dress set him apart. Like me he rose early and when still in his dressing gown he would make us tea. He was very formal shaking hands each morning. As I sat at the kitchen table he would then go up to his dressing room before returning in full splendour. He wore a purple finely embroidered smoking jacket and on his head a fez made of the same material complete with a tassel that danced and pranced as he moved. I had never seen anyone wear a fez before or since and I had no idea what prompted him to wear it. I was too shy to ask. Had he spent time in north Africa? Although he was friendly he rarely spoke and yet I felt he welcomed some male company. I never saw him leave the house during daylight hours and yet I learnt later that each night after my sister and I were in bed he went to the local pub and apparently had a bit of a reputation as a boozer.

What particularly drew me to him was his passion for collecting. The house was full of strange artefacts drawn from across the world including Japanese drawings on rice paper, tribal art from Polynesia and scantily dressed art nouveau figures, but his real fascination was for stamps. These were contained in rows of leather covered albums all neatly listed in alphabetical order. Apparently he had one of the largest collections in the country. I have no idea where he acquired them from but each morning there were more that needed to be painstakingly fixed in the appropriate album. I learnt more about different parts of the world watching Monty than I ever did at school. Where are all those stamps today? They must be worth a fortune today. Were they sold as a collection, broken up or still lying in a cupboard somewhere ignored and forgotten?

Monty's other passion was collecting butterflies. Stored in military precision in glass fronted cabinets, they were stunningly beautiful but made me feel slightly queasy. They needed to be free and fluttering not skewered in airless cabinets. Again how did he acquire them? He told me many were from far flung parts of the world. I wish I had been more confident in asking him, but although friendly enough I sensed he did not welcome my prying. So I imagined him as some sort of explorer travelling the world, but now there is no-one to ask and Monty remains an enigma, a mystery, his life story like so many floating away and forgotten. In many ways he was a larger than life character, but every life is interesting if you are prepared to glimpse behind the defensive screen that we all tend to erect when meeting someone new.

Chapter 21

It Ain't Half Cold, Mum

Every child who lived through the winter of 1947 shivers at the very thought of it. Memories of chilblains and frozen feet as snow came over the tops of wellington boots. What had seemed magical with the first snowfall now invaded every part of life. Coming home from school perished only to find the electricity cut off. Then later toasting bread for tea in front of a two-barred electric fire that failed even to take the chill off the room. Then early to bed in an attempt to get warm with the help of a stone hot water bottle that soon cooled. Then waking in the morning with the windows frozen inside. Getting dressed under the bedclothes and then down for breakfast only to find the coke boiler has gone out overnight. The cold was unrelenting. It gnawed away making everyone tetchy and grumpy. When would it ever end?

Snow had started falling in December but this was just a dress rehearsal of what was to come. The cold persisted but it was on 23rd January that the real trouble started. Within days huge drifts had formed closing roads, whilst abandoned cars and lorries disappeared under a white blanket. The heavy snow also led to the shutdown of much of the railway network and the cutting of supplies to the power stations.

Any hopes I had of having a few days off school were soon dashed. Dragged and complaining much as I had on my first day, my mother said that a little snow was not going to interrupt my education. A little snow! In parts the snow came up almost to my waist. Still we struggled on. At last we arrived wet, bedraggled and freezing, to find that only a handful of students and just one teacher had made it in. We were sent home. What a victory and for a few days my mother relented. Perhaps it was a generation thing but we were all taught back then never to take the easy option. A harsh lesson but one that generally served our generation well over the years.

The winds howled in from the east. There was apparently a depression centred over Scandinavia bringing further heavy snowfalls to the south east. Then a deeper overall depression took hold over the country. Already there were food shortages with vegetables being frozen in the ground and transportation severely affected. By the end of the month the snow had spread to all parts of the country with temperatures dropping to minus twenty degrees centigrade.

February is frequently the most depressing month of the year. We long for the appearance of Spring but in 1947 even the snowdrops and aconites were covered in a blanket of snow and ice. Welcome to one of the coldest months ever recorded in Britain. For two nights only did the temperature haul itself above freezing. For almost the entire month the sun failed to appear in England. Wales also recorded one of its gloomiest months and yet in Scotland the weather was dry and sunny. Perishingly cold but the sun helped present a picture card landscape. By the end of February the ferry between Dover and Ostend was suspended due to ice. Europe was also shivering. Snow in England was recorded on twenty six days. Villages were cut off, hundreds of main roads were blocked again and the whole country was in danger of grinding to a complete halt. Factories and offices were shut and production was dangerously low. Snow in the big cities was constantly cleared in an attempt to keep life moving. Department stores were packed. Not with paying customers, just people trying to get warm. There were reports of soaring levels of shoplifting.

The misery tightened with declining fuel supplies. The limited stockpiles of coal at depots froze solid and could not be moved. The military were called in to help and German prisoners of war were co-opted to lend a hand. Some power stations had to shut down completely. The fledgling television station was shut down whilst wireless output was restricted. The Third Programme was taken off air completely whilst the Home Service and the Light Programme had their schedules reduced. There was little enough pleasure to be had and now even that was being controlled. The minister for Fuel and Power, Manny Shinwell now made himself even more unpopular by cutting electricity supplies to industry completely. For six hours a day there were no domestic supplies either. Resentment and anger grew and still across the country people stamped their feet and piled on even more layers of clothes in a vain attempt to keep warm. Queues at shops grew, tempers frayed. Cattle caught in snowdrifts died as did thousand of chickens. Pneumatic drills were used to extract vegetables but when potatoes were rationed for the first time a mixture of rage and helplessness swept the country.

Surely after two months it was time for winter to loosen its grip but March brought even greater problems. Pipes continued to burst all over the country and plumbers were able to name their price. A feeling not far short of despair took hold in many quarters. The country was almost bankrupt, there was trouble fermenting in India and Palestine, but all of this paled under the continuing barrage of snow and ice.

The beginning of March saw further heavy snowfalls with drifts up to twenty feet in Scotland. The roads throughout the country were rutted and treacherous. The hospitals were kept busy by road accidents and people falling over on icy pavements. 5th March witnessed the worst ever blizzard to hit Britain and the country ground to a halt with food supplies stuck in ports and blocked roads. Until now even children were becoming fed up with the snowy conditions but this fresh fall was spectacular and something to be remembered. The conditions quickly became too difficult for them to use their sledges and yet still the snow came. Within a couple of days there was a sudden rise in temperature in the south west of England, causing a rapid thaw triggering a new source of concern with widespread flooding. Further north the milder air prompted further heavy snowfalls. By mid March Durham recorded over eighty inches of snow, a record for Great Britain.

Within days a deepening depression from the Atlantic brought heavy rain and howling gales. With winds approaching ninety miles an hour trees were felled and dykes breached. It was as if Britain had been singled out for punishment. Those household pipes that had held out so far now burst. Many houses were flooded adding to the misery. Parts of east Anglia looked like a vast lake. In London the Thames and the River Lea burst their banks. For centuries the Thames Valley had given way to its snakelike progress of its iconic river but had seldom witnessed such severe flooding. Water rushed into the centre of Windsor flooding homes and the main shopping area. If anything matters were worse in Nottingham as the River Trent burst its banks. Following the heaviest rainfall in half a century the river levels rose ominously, finally bursting its banks on 18th March and causing the worst flooding in the Trent Valley that anyone could remember. The Clifton Colliery was cut off and people had to be rescued by boat. Now even the cold seemed preferable to the all encompassing wet and damp. Furniture and carpets were ruined and many were not insured. So far 1947 had been a disaster for much of the population. Still the waters rose as high as the upper floor of houses in West Bridgford.

Further north Long Eaton succumbed. Thousands of acres across the country were now under water. High spring tides conspired to spread its malign misery to thousands more. As the rivers slowly subsided in the south west so they rose in Yorkshire and Lincolnshire. The Derwent, Wharfe and Ouse all burst their banks. Sandbags offered little protection and although the army was brought in they could only look on as over one hundred thousand homes were invaded by the foul smelling water.

The floods made the international news and food parcels were sent from Australia and Canada. Gradually the waters subsided leaving the horrible job of clearing up the soggy mess. The extreme weather of that winter further weakened the country's economic situation, but it is a time remembered by all who lived through it. There have been savage winters since but none so long or severe. Gradually flood defences have been improved. Now surely it was time to look forward.

By July memories of the savage winter best remembered for the snow and floods had almost been forgotten with the excitement at the prospect of a Royal wedding.

In July the engagement of Princess Elizabeth to Prince Philip of Greece was announced. Once again there was to be a grand showpiece event for the public to look forward to. The eagle-eyed may have realised that the developing romance was progressing when the future Queen was bridesmaid to her lady-in-waiting, the honourable Mrs. Vicary Gibbs. After the wedding at St. Margaret's church, Westminster, the reception was held in the River Room at the Savoy. This was the first time that the entire Royal family had been seen together in a London hotel. Outside, the entrance was crowded with photographers, but only one of their number was allowed to photograph the reception. When the photographs were released one pictured the princess standing alongside a good looking naval officer on this, their first public appearance together. A generally enthusiastic pro-royalty public approved and anxiously awaited developments. A poll in the Sunday Pictorial asked readers 'should Elizabeth marry Philip?' Sixty-two percent were in favour, with thirty-two against. Not all were so impressed, however. Despite his excellent record during the war there were problems. Philip was extremely poor and his German background was underscored by his three sisters all being married to Germans. None of them were invited to the wedding. Never mind, he had been educated in Britain and spoke English without a hint of an accent, despite having been born in Greece, and he had become a naturalised British citizen. He looked like a film star and was no chinless wonder. He would do.

How to project the wedding was causing concern. An extravagant display of wealth was certain to attract criticism in a time of ongoing austerity, and yet a royal wedding demanded a certain pomp and ceremony. Over 2,000 guests were invited to the service at Westminster Abbey and London's hotels were full to bursting. The barman in the American Bar at the Savoy offered a 'wedding bells' cocktail and gala dinners were planned at all the leading hotels and restaurants throughout the West End. At Claridges, royalty from across Europe were falling over each other. In her last public appearance before the wedding, Princess Elizabeth appeared at the Flower Ball held at the Savoy. Jean Nicol (admittedly something of a sycophant) reported that she 'had never seen her look prettier, her hair longer and softer than usual and her petal skin glowing like a pink pearl'.

No public holiday had been granted for the wedding, so the young princess was astonished to see huge crowds gathered round the palace as she looked down from a second floor window. It was a grey, damp morning and people had slept outside on divan mattresses and in sleeping bags. The wedding morning is normally a stressful time for brides and so it proved for the princess. Her dress, designed by Norman Hartnell and worked on by no fewer than 350 women was stunning, but then disaster – the Russian tiara that had been worn by her grandmother at her wedding snapped. The court jeweller was summoned and a hasty temporary repair undertaken.

The procession of the bridesmaids, including Princess Margaret, set off to the abbey. So did Philip, fortified by a stiff drink. He was accompanied by his cousin, the Marquis of Milford Haven, who was his best man. The previous day, Philip had renounced his Greek and Danish titles and on the morning of the wedding had been appointed His Royal Highness, the Duke of Edinburgh. As the bride set off from the gates of Buckingham Palace with her father in the Irish state coach, the crowds roared their support. The BBC had fifty-five microphones positioned along the route, with television and newsreel cameras also recording the scene. It was estimated that some 200 million people worldwide listened to the radio broadcast which was covered by commentators, including Wynford Vaughan-Thomas, Richard Dimbleby and Frank Gillard.

During the wedding service, the Archbishop of York became rather carried away by suggesting that the wedding was, in essence, little different by those carried out in many a humble village church. The major part of the service was conducted by the Archbishop of Canterbury, Geoffrey Fisher. A rather dry, but godly man. Unusually for a leading cleric, he was also a committed Freemason as was Prince Philip from 1952.

Over in the River Room at the Savoy, banks of chairs were arranged in front of a tiny, flickering television set for those who had been unable to secure a seat along the route. Waiters ducked and dived, carrying trays of coffees and cocktails, in an attempt not to obstruct the distorted pictures being transmitted from the abbey. The newly married couple travelled back to the palace in a glass coach. There were 150 guests for the wedding breakfast, who enjoyed a family themed menu starting with Filet de Sole Mountbatten. Certainly no-one was able to accuse the couple of embarking on a lavish honeymoon. There were no luxury yachts or Caribbean beaches for them to look forward to. Instead, they travelled to Waterloo station in an open landau with hot water bottles at their feet. Maybe three's a crowd, but the princess's favourite corgi went too. The honeymoon was spent at Broadlands, the country estate of the Mountbatten family. Doubtless, like most of us at a similar time in our lives, they pondered what the future held in store for them. Later in the month, a curious public queued round St. James to get a close up look at the bridal gown. It was on display together with over 2,000 gifts the couple had received from around the world.

The celebrations over, a collective gloom settled in. People had become disillusioned. Record numbers were making enquiries about emigrating. South Africa and Australia were favoured destinations. The middle classes felt particularly hard done by. Most felt that their standard of living had declined when compared to pre-war days. The gap between them and the working class had closed, whilst the wealthy, despite increased taxation, appeared outwardly unaffected. It was estimated that ten percent of the middle class buying power had been forcefully transferred to lower paid earners. H. V. Morton spoke for many when he said 'England had become a society where things moved steadily towards Communism'. However put upon the middle classes were feeling, few surely could have objected to the school leaving age being raised to fifteen. Many were initially pleased when the chancellor of the exchequer, Hugh Dalton, was forced to resign after leaking details of his budget to a lobby journalist. He was succeeded by the 'holier than thou' Stafford Cripps, and middle England realised that for them life was not about to get any easier.

The end of the Raj, with the partition of India in 1947, was another reminder that Britain's place in the world was being diluted. The empire on which 'the sun never set' was beginning to unravel. Partition in Palestine was also underway. British military losses in the holy land had led to a new wave of anti-Semitism in Britain. This loss of power and control was having a strange effect on the nation's psyche. We had won the war and yet we were now seemingly in retreat. Many were experiencing a collective loss of confidence whilst the government continued with its radical reforms and off-loaded long held assets.

Chapter 22

Say aaah

It was a look that my mother gave me occasionally and I knew exactly what it meant. Don't say anything. We were standing at a bus stop in Tottenham Court Road in central London. Standing next to me was the first black man I had ever seen in the flesh. He smiled and said hello. Shyly I replied. He towered above me and was wearing grey trousers and a blue Olympic blazer. My mother need not have thought I was going to make some insensitive remark. I thought this young man looked like a god from ancient times. Later I found out that he was Arthur Wint who went on to win the gold medal for the four hundred metres at the Wembley Olympics. He then added a silver for the eight hundred metres. As a sports mad youngster I was furious with myself that I had not asked for his autograph.

There were three major events in that summer of 1948, each of which are remembered still, although in retrospect the Olympic games were the least important. Firstly on 2nd June the troopship the Empire Windrush docked in Tilbury bringing five hundred and ten immigrants from Jamaica, thus starting the gradual change towards Britain becoming a multi-racial society. A month later on July 5th saw the launching of the revolutionary National Health Service. These two events witnessed major changes to British life, but not before encountering massive problems which in a sense still drag on today.

Although it was estimated that there were only about thirty thousand non-whites living in Great Britain at the time, the arrival of the Empire Windrush filled government officials with alarm. A colonial office official warned that a disorganised rush of West Indian immigrants would be a disaster. Unemployment in the East End of London was already rising and attitudes to black people had changed. The initial relatively warm welcome given to black GIs had hardened significantly. The old British antagonism to anyone different from themselves had resurfaced with a vengeance. The colonial secretary Arthur Creech Jones acknowledged the rights of the men to come to Britain and with a misplaced confidence peculiar to British politicians predicted 'I do not think that a similar mass movement will take place again.' He added that these men would not 'last a single winter in England.' Despite his confidence efforts were made to delay the arrival of the ship to give time for the authorities to find jobs for the men. Ideally these were to be away from London and the men to be dispersed to different outlying areas. There was only one female aboard the Windrush. Averill Wanchove was an attractive twenty five year old seamstress who was liable to be deported back to the West Indies. Discovered a week after the ship set sail her case was taken up by Nancy Cunard the shipping heiress who stated her intention to look after the young stowaway.

So they arrived, these hundreds of men all smartly dressed in what they supposed was the British manner. Smart albeit lightweight suits and trilby hats. In a change of plan many were housed by the London county council in Brixton which over the years became a centre for the West Indian community. It was Labour politicians who appeared most anxious about immigration. In a letter to Prime Minister Atlee they wrote: 'This country may become an open reception centre for immigrants not selected in respect of health, education, training, character, customs and above all whether assimilation is possible or not.' The letter went on to say that 'An influx of coloured people domiciled here is likely to impair the harmony, strength and cohesion of our public and social life and to cause discord and unhappiness among all concerned.' Unfortunately they were right and by the end of June serious racial riots had broken out.

Living in Brixton young Iris Chapple was ten years old when the first West Indians arrived in her neighbourhood. She remembers that Brixton was already home to a wide variety of nationalities which added to the vibrancy of the area. Her mother rented their home from a Hungarian. Already used to the smells of paprika and other spices not used in British cooking, she welcomed the arrival of these black men who shouted greetings to her in the street. Tantalising new smells of cooking accompanied by loud music that was not welcomed by the neighbours. For Iris the music was strange but exciting. She was already a talented dancer with a natural sense of rhythm often denied to British people. On a warm summer's night she would listen and dance to the music booming out. Later Iris was going to become a professional dancer spending several happy years as a Windmill girl. She was warned about becoming too friendly with these black men. Opinion spiralled from a friendly welcome to outright antagonism. Soon KBW (Keep Britain White) posters started appearing. Now even their choice of fruit and vegetables were criticised. Mangoes and sweet potatoes condemned without even being tried by the white population. Wild stories of the sexual excesses of these black men were circulated. Because so few West Indian women had arrived there was certainly a mixing with local girls underway that caused great resentment. New arrivals led to overcrowding and many local residents were moving out. 'No blacks, Irish or dogs' became a familiar sight on 'to let' signs. It had not taken long for racial disharmony to set in and it was going to take decades, outwardly at least, for matters to improve.

In the days when it was possible to see a doctor and even receive a home visit, many who were youngsters in the 1940s remember the cold feel of the stethoscope as they battled with one of common child illnesses. Mumps, whooping cough and chicken pox hit very hard. Life became muddled and if badly effected as temperatures rose and days feeling rotten merged. Our Scottish Doctor Wilson would arrive in his Austin Seven. Drink plenty of water was his cure for most ailments and resist scratching your spots when chicken pox struck. The cost of a visit was five shillings and because he never appeared rushed once downstairs he would enjoy a cup of tea with my mother. But there were changes afoot. Radical changes which would affect every household across the country.

The National Health Service (NHS) came into being on 5th July 1948. The man destined to implement this radical overhaul of our health care was a chubby charismatic class warrior. Despite a pronounced lisp Aneurin (Nye) Bevan was a formidable driven politician. A superb orator and capable of turning on considerable charm. He fought a long and bitter battle with the medical establishment. To win them over he was forced to 'stuff the consultants' mouths with gold'. This enabled them to maintain some pay beds in hospitals shortly to be taken over by the State.

The transformation to a State run system involved a number of key elements. Most important was the decision that care was to be free and universal. Costs would be borne by central government rather than insurance. All hospitals would be covered by the scheme although consultants would be able through the pay bed agreement to combine their private practice with working for the NHS. GPs were no longer allowed to sell their practices and patients were able to change their doctor if required. Now everyone in Britain was entitled to universal access to free medical care. Within a couple of months ninety seven percent of the population had registered with an NHS doctor. The costs of the service were to be financed through central taxation and hospitals nationalised. The cost of medicines was also covered by the scheme and were to be dispensed free by chemists.

Within weeks it became obvious that costs were rising way beyond initial estimates. Some doctors were dispensing antibiotics like sweets from a corner shop. The scope of the scheme included free spectacles, false teeth and artificial limbs. But it was the bill for drugs that appeared out of control. In two years the overspend compared to the budget amounted to almost thirty million pounds. Despite this Bevan refused to introduce prescription charges stating that 'It would greatly reduce the prestige of the service.' Mobile clinics were sent to schools and it was among the young that health improved the most. No doubt despite the huge costs the NHS was deemed by the public to be a great success. Unable to resist his loathing of the Conservatives whom Bevan described as scum, he would have approved of a doctor who stated 'The local aristocracy has joined the NHS and they wait their turn in the surgery with the rest.'

Away from the class wars there was a huge worry about one illness that had the power to devastate children's lives. Poliomyelitis, known commonly as infantile paralysis, caused alarm amongst parents worried about their children. The trouble was the initial symptoms were similar to other children's diseases with headache, vomiting and a general feeling of weakness. I remember a boy at my school whose left arm hung flopping uncontrollably as he tried to join in playing football. It was a constant reminder to why my mother seemed so concerned whenever I developed childish symptoms. In an attempt to placate rising concern an article in Picture Post sought to calm nerves, but the harrowing photographs of stricken children did little to alleviate worries. The article, which was written by the well known journalist Fyfe Robertson rather than a medical expert, also smacked of propaganda rather than informed medical facts.

The article headed 'No need for panic' stressed that the lack of reliable information and statistics had led to a state of unwarranted alarm. He stated that there had always been outbreaks normally experienced in the late summer or early autumn. Normally about six to eight hundred cases a year. He admitted that the current outbreak was likely to register record yet still comparatively low figures. He maintained that most cases recorded were mild and in any event only a tiny proportion of the population were affected. He further maintained that two thirds of those showing symptoms suffered no paralysis. This surely hardly comforted parents reading the article because on the page was a graphic photo of a youngster entombed in an iron lung. Robertson went on to state that for every one hundred sufferers fifty recovered completely. Thirty were left with what he described as minor muscular defects. Hardly lightening the mood he told us that fifteen would be permanently disabled whilst five would die. Any parent reading the article to this point it seems would be rather more worried if not panicked by what they had read.

Robertson visited the Western hospital in Fulham which was the main receiving hospital for acute cases. He referred to the dedicated staff and their young charges whose patient and happy acceptance of their disabilities was apparently moving and merciful. Again there were photographs of a young boy having an ice bath and the acknowledgment that doctors just didn't know if there was any value to be gained by physiotherapy. On an opposite page a young boy learned to walk with the help of an iron support. A caption informed us that his paralysed leg would not improve any more. Finally the advice for parents was to insist on personal cleanliness. Wash hands regularly. Keeping flies away from food is surely just common sense but did it really stop Polio? Children should get proper rest and sleep as fatigue seemed to increase the risk of infection. Having taken these basic precautions the reader was encouraged to forget all about the illness as winter approached. This strange piece of journalism surely created more doubts than solutions and added to the alarm of parents.

Away from concerns about children's health, eighty five thousand people held their collective breath. In the sweltering July heat they were packed into Wembley stadium to witness the opening ceremony of the London Olympic Games. They need not have worried for the King, dressed in naval uniform, declared the games open without the hint of the stutter that made these public appearances such a trial for him. There was a massive sense of anticipation as they awaited the arrival of the Olympic torch. There had been rumours that it might be carried by the

Duke of Edinburgh, although surely the stuffy officials at Buckingham Palace would veto any such idea.

Now Sir Malcolm Sargent looking smooth, silky and slightly satanic, stepped forward to conduct the massed bands of the Brigade of Guards. They played Rudyard Kipling's 'Non nobis, domine' to music by Roger Quilter. It was a moment of national pride and throughout the crowd a few tears were shed before, to an initial hush, the torch entered the arena. The bearer was certainly blond but much taller than Prince Philip. The athlete chosen was John Mark. Even Adolf Hitler would have approved. Over six feet in height his blond hair caught the light as he made his way round the running track to a raised dais. He was a junior doctor at St. Mary's hospital in Paddington and his selection was certainly appropriate coming just three weeks after the launching of the NHS. A Cambridge blue, at the quarter mile he covered a full lap and climbing the steps he stood motionless for a moment before lighting the flame that would burn for the duration of the games.

Just two days after the opening of the Olympic games and following the arrival of the Empire Windrush there was serious racial rioting in Liverpool. It was a bank holiday weekend and the steamy heatwave continued. Railway stations were crammed with people heading for the coast. Most ports in Britain did have black residents who were generally successfully absorbed into the general population. Tension had been growing in Liverpool regarding black workers apparently undercutting the locals by accepting lower wages. This combined with the unusual heat helped create the recipe for trouble. White gangs attacked rooming houses used by black seamen. The police moved in and made one arrest - a black seaman. Worse was to come the following day. Hostels and cafes were attacked. This time there were six arrests, all black. As the situation worsened there were over thirty arrests made, again all of them black. There were complaints about police brutality and the planting of weapons on black men to help gain convictions. Neither in the press nor in the courts was any real attempt made to understand the real reasons for the violence. On a wonderful summer's weekend when the country should have been celebrating it signalled an ominous future of rising racial tension.

The London Olympics was awarded in a sense by default. The Game's reputation had been tarnished by the overt Nazi propaganda of the 1936

Olympics held in Berlin. The 1940 Games had been scheduled to take place in Tokyo. There were severe misgivings that they too would be a launch-pad for another aggressive military regime. Worse, dark rumours spread that bribes had been made to members of the Olympic Committee (IOC). Holidays and other inducements were offered. Tokyo was issued with a warning that their games could be cancelled. Luckily this threat was overtaken by events. Japan was engaged in a very expensive war with China and so with their financial problems mounting they withdrew their right to stage the Olympics.

Subsequently the war intervened and initially in 1944 the next Games were awarded to Helsinki, but it was decided that the Finnish capital had suffered too much war damage to its infrastructure to be able to stage a major sporting event. It was then agreed that London should take on the challenge. Despite the widespread damage inflicted on the city it still had sufficient suitable venues with Wembley stadium providing an iconic setting for major events. These were to include both the opening and closing ceremonies together with football and equestrian events. Earls Court was designated to host weightlifting, wrestling and basketball. Away from London the Herne Bay Velodrome would organise the cycling events whilst the Thames at Henley provided a wonderful backdrop for the rowing.

Major problems were not confined to the venues. Where were over one thousand competitors, their coaches and officials going to stay? Anyone looking for a luxury break was going to be disappointed. Accommodation ranged from passable to frankly basic. Schools, office buildings even barracks were designated. No single suites, more likely dormitories with rows of beds stretching out. Hardly ideal for elite athletes expected to compete on the world stage. Most were also not about to enjoy a gourmet experience. Meals were well organised but basic. Teams had to eat together at set times, or if unable to attend request a packed lunch or supper. Some food was supplied by commercial restaurants. They were allowed a budget of twenty five shillings per day for each athlete. In addition they were allowed to run snack bars for profit. To cater for so many types of food was a huge challenge. Veeraswamy, London's oldest Indian restaurant made daily deliveries to Pinner county school for the Indian competitors. The thirty competitors from China enjoyed food prepared by Ley On's Chinese restaurant in Wardour Street.

Somehow against all the odds the games unfolded with increasing confidence. British organisation was asserting itself. A fleet of vans and cars was despatched daily to take athletes and officials to the various venues. A nod to modern technology was evident with the introduction of photo finishes in the sprints recorded on camera. Television, although still in its infancy in Britain, was there to record the events. The marketing gurus of today would shake their heads in disbelief at the sums paid for TV and advertising rights. One thousand pounds was the figure paid by the BBC for broadcasting for both TV and radio. Few in Britain owned a television set so the radio coverage was almost more important with over six hundred staff covering the events. Sponsorship was also still in its infancy. Two hundred and fifty pounds was enough to secure the right to feature the five ringed Olympic logo in your advertising. Cigarette brands like Craven A leapt at the opportunity. Seemingly almost everyone over the age of fifteen smoked as did those younger given the chance. The Guinness company proudly proclaimed that Guinness was good for you and countless other popular brands joined in the advertising bonanza.

The first day of competition gave a hint of where women's sport was heading. It was still felt by some that any form of physical sport for women was un-ladylike. They were fighting a losing battle as the first medals awarded on the opening day were for the women's discus. Previously the javelin had been allowed but now the discus and the shot-put had been added. Soon huge eastern European ladies would be a regular sight at athletics events. For the moment the competitors still did their best, but the distances they achieved were way below what was to follow over the coming years.

My parents' next door neighbour owned a television set albeit with a tiny screen. I realised that Miss Wanklyn was unusual but I thought my parents were unkind about her. She dressed in thick tweeds no matter how hot it was. Thick woollen stockings too and brogue shoes. When out on a walk she carried a stick and wore a trilby hat. She had a friend called Enid who visited regularly. She was like a little mouse, all frills and bows. As I watched the flickering screen being transmitted from only a few miles away, they served me tea and gave me cake. They were so kind and I really liked them both. It was years before I understood what my parents found so amusing about them. My mum and dad, like most people at the time, were surely guilty of the British sin of ridiculing people different from themselves. At the end of the first week of competition I went with my dad to watch the marathon runners on their route back to Wembley. The roads were lined with spectators and every runner was given a hearty cheer. The loudest was reserved for the British runner Tom Richards. He was well placed when he passed us and went on to win silver, coming second behind Delfo Cabrera of Argentina. We waited for the stragglers to pass us, their faces contorted with pain but determined to finish and all of them still cheered on their way.

Each Olympic games throws up one outstanding athlete that tends to be remembered decades later. This was certainly the case in London where 'the flying Dutchwoman' swept the board. I remember seeing her on the Pathe News. Blonde and leggy, eclipsing all-comers. Voted as 'female athlete of the century' in 1939, many thought that Fanny Blankers-Koen would be too old to fight off a clutch of young athletes at Wembley. The mother of two children and reputed to be pregnant again, rules established she was only allowed to compete in four events rather than the six she had qualified for. She decided to confine herself to the hundred metres blue ribbon sprint showpiece as well as the two hundred metres. In addition she was entered for the eighty metres hurdles and the four by four hundred metre relay.

Two sprinters in the 1946 European championships were subsequently found to be men. However, there was no doubting Fanny's femininity despite the old prejudices about women exerting themselves unduly being un-ladylike. She eased through the heats and semi-final of the hundred metres, but by now the heatwave had given way to torrential rain. The cinder track was covered in puddles. It was a no contest. Her strange style of leaning back as she ran in no way impeded her. She won easing down by a full three yards with the British runner Dorothy Manley coming second. The next day the weather was wetter still. Her main rival in the eighty metres hurdles was Maureen Gardner, a nineteen year old British girl. The press went into overdrive convinced a British victory would crown Gardner the golden girl of the games. For once Fanny had a poor start, perhaps still getting accustomed to the new starting blocks being used for the first time at the Olympics. By midway the two women were locked together and that is how it stayed. At the last moment Blankers-Koen threw herself at the tape. A photo finish. It seemed to take an age before Fanny was announced as the winner by a whisker.

Stating that she was feeling very tired Fanny entered the two hundred metres expecting to be trounced. Actually she decimated her rivals in a superb display of sustained sprinting. Despite her physical and mental exhaustion she was determined not to let her three friends down in the relay. By the time she was handed the baton on the final leg the Dutch had fallen back to fourth place. She ran as she had never run before. Inspired, with her long hair caught in the breeze, she started gaining. The whole stadium was on their feet. They were witnessing athletic history. Astonishingly Fanny edged her way to take the tape as the winner yet again. She was not too old or delicate. She was a role model for women in a changing world. Supremely talented yet modest. She had proved all the doubters wrong and gave oxygen to the thought that in life anything is possible.

It was with some sadness that at last after all the drama and excitement the arena was cleared for the final ceremony. Days of effort and achievement, drama, joy and tears were over. The Olympic flag was lowered and the flame extinguished. It proved to be the last truly amateur games before the money men moved in. The event had been generally rated a success. Well organised on a small budget. Slightly self-effacing. A very British success. For me and millions of other youngsters it increased our interest in playing and watching sporting events.

Chapter 23

Owzat

For many children sport equated to standing around on a windswept hockey or football pitch feeling thoroughly miserable. This culminated in the horrors of the school's annual sports day. Running, jumping, straining every sinew and cheered on by doting parents. The humiliation of coming last even in the egg and spoon race remain a seared memory, but for the majority an interest in sport developed early in life. Life is a great leveller and so it was that often those who were non-academic excelled at cricket or netball.

Generally it is reckoned that it is boys who are most likely to be infected by the sports bug but the girls were not about to be sidelined. For every girl like Jean Sporle who loathed sports there were those who were actively and happily involved and they were not part of the 'jolly hockey sticks' brigade. Girls who regularly attended ballet classes were often able to use that balance and grace to good effect. After the war Britain was well blessed with a number of regional ice rinks. Ice skating was a sport where the girls normally shone compared to their clumsy brothers. Ice rinks from Paisley and Aberdeen in Scotland to Streatham and Brighton further south, these venues were a perfect meeting place for young people. Most featured snack bars where it was possible to have a cup of tea and compare bruises. Skates were available for hire and it did not take long to discover that staying upright was not as easy as it looked. Lesley Taylor regularly travelled to Nottingham feeling rather smug wearing her smart white skates that she still has today. She would join the other good skaters in the centre of the rink, leaving the beginners desperately trying to stay upright and clinging on to the rails at the side.

With so few cars on the roads even after the war had ended it was a common sight to see groups of kids playing football or cricket on the street or even deserted bomb sites. Like now football was a national obsession helped by the professional game starting up again. From Roker Park to Craven Cottage, many youngsters were taken by their dads to see their first game. Often passed down to the very front so that the youngster had a clear view. The excitement was thrilling, you became part of a live theatre shouting and moaning as the game unfolded. You were surrounded by an army of fans. A sea of flat caps, scarves and the clack-clack of rattles which were still in common use and helped create part of the unique atmosphere of match day.

There was a huge pent up demand for any form of spectator sport and crowds swelled to record attendances. Even the top stars like Stanley Matthews and Len Shackleton had their wages restricted to a maximum of twelve pounds a week. Many of the top players arrived at the ground by bus. These were not the days of multi-millionaire prima donnas who strut their stuff today. The first post-war cup final in 1946 attracted a crowd of one hundred thousand to Wembley between Derby County and Charlton Athletic. A one-all draw after ninety minutes, Derby went on to score three goals in extra time.

Sports broadcasting was becoming ever more popular and those doing the commentaries became almost more famous than the stars and the events they were covering. Foremost amongst these was Raymond Glendenning whose breathless and excitable delivery conjured a vivid picture in the listener's mind. Unfortunately some of his descriptions were not always accurate, particularly when covering horse racing. Here he was quite capable of announcing the wrong winner before subsequently correcting the result without the hint of an apology. He also covered every FA cup final from 1946 to 1963. With his horn-rimmed glasses and handlebar moustache, over the years he became something of a national treasure. He was probably at his best covering boxing. I was allowed to stay up to listen to the fight between Bruce Woodcock and the American Joe Baksi in April 1947. The crowd at Haringey paid between five shillings and ten guineas to see the British hopeful who was knocked down twice in the first round and again in the second before the fight was stopped in the seventh to save Woodcock from more damage. Listening to the big fights was a regular treat for me and I still remember the inter-round summaries by the rather grand sounding W. Barrington Dalby.

A strange very English sporting event took place each year on the River Thames. Crowds flocked to the towpath to watch two crews representing the ancient universities of Oxford and Cambridge. Jean Sporle who lived in Hammersmith only a couple of streets back from the river went each year. Londoners have always embraced the event despite very few of them attending either of the universities or even visiting the spired cities. Back in the 1940s this did not diminish the excitement. Many wore rosettes of dark or light blue to indicate their support. The crews shot by to raucous cheering, particularly if the race was run whilst the pubs were open. Once again it was a radio commentator whose voice became synonymous with the race. In which other country would millions have tuned into hear John Snage say slowly and repeatedly 'in out, in out' as the race continued on its journey from Mortlake to Putney.

Perhaps it was cycling that was enjoyed equally by boys and girls. It encouraged a sense of adventure and exploring new places away from home. With the roads still largely deserted it was a pastime that could be enjoyed with a group of friends or alone. With a drink and a packed lunch safely stowed away in your saddle bag the open road was yours. Of course the type of bike you rode was important. For boys it had to be drop handlebars and the more gears the better, otherwise trying to keep up was a nightmare. The poster boy for cycling was Reg Harris who became the world sprint champion in 1947 before going on to win two Olympic silver medals the following year. Herne Hill Velodrome in south London was the centre of serious race riding and like other sports attracted vast crowds.

Before so many schools sold off their playing fields it was not just the private schools that were able to offer sporting facilities. Even inner city schools normally had a netball court, whilst improvised cricket and football matches were held on tarmac playgrounds. Teachers encouraged rising stars, gaining much prestige by beating rival schools.

Watching young boys playing their first organised football game usually involves them all chasing after the ball until eventually they begin to understand the responsibilities for each position and the games become less frenetic and more structured. Most of us have a limited ability even in our favoured sport but it often became obvious at an early stage who the future star performers would be. Whatever the sport those who are really talented always appear to have more time than the rest of us. What a great leveller life can be as the classroom dunce suddenly becomes envied for his natural sporting skills. Of course there are those rare birds who appear to effortlessly glide through life by being both really clever and talented at a whole variety of sports. Uncannily this rare breed also tends to be very good looking as well. It's just not fair!

Cricket can soon become a game of sore ribs and broken fingers when the leather ball is first introduced to youngsters for the first time. It would be wrong to think that it was only boys who endured pain in pursuit of their favourite sport. Hockey played by an enthusiastic group of girls can be frightening and dangerous. It is reckoned that mixed-sex hockey often ends up with someone being carted off to hospital for running repairs.

Meanwhile the attendances at even minor sporting events continued to soar during the 1940s. With almost no television coverage it was necessary to attend live events to be able to see the stars of the day. My first visit to a test match was in 1946. I caught an early bus with my dad, but by the time we reached Lords crowds stretched right round from the nursery end to the main gates. I was convinced we would not get in but gradually the crowd shuffled forward. Once through the turnstile we bought a score card for threepence and made our way to the nearest stand. My memories of the day are vague but I did see my namesake Len Hutton bat as well as the glamour boy Dennis Compton. The Indian attack contained wily spinners but two years later I saw one of the strongest Australian teams ever to visit England. I had hoped to see the famous Don Bradman bat but seeing the Aussie fast bowlers was exciting enough. They reminded me of the American GIs, they looked bigger and fitter than our boys. Ray Lindwall bowled so quickly that their wicket keeper Don Tallon stood halfway back to the boundary as the ball thudded into his gloves. Live sport is like live theatre without a script, unpredictable and spellbinding for a youngster.

Crowd behaviour at sporting events was so different to today. Kids watching football matches remembered a charged partisan atmosphere but no swearing or obscene chanting. Plenty of booing and cheering but generally a friendly atmosphere. The contrast at first class cricket matches was even more apparent. No singing, no fancy dress, everything was rather serious with just a ripple of applause for a good shot or fielding. Neither did fielders throw themselves about and often just stuck out a boot to save a boundary. Generally there was no talking in between overs. A sense of calm and the noise of leather on willow. It seems strange to us now but there was a huge gulf between the amateur and professional players. Social differences still mattered and were emphasised, even on that first score card I bought that day at Lords. My father explained that the players with their initials in front of their surnames were amateurs.

Presumably people with a private income who did not get paid for playing. Conversely the pros had their initials printed after their name. In some counties the professionals entered by a separate door and there were even segregated changing rooms. The system was underscored by the annual 'Gentlemen against Players' match held annually at Lords. Astonishingly this fixture tottered on into the 1960s.

Rugby union remained the most amateur of games at least in England. In Wales there were stories of boots stuffed with notes for their stars, but nothing so tawdry for their English counterparts. There was not even any form of league as ostensibly all the matches played were 'friendlies'. This in no way reduced the passion or physicality of the encounters. Even the elite clubs confined training to a couple of nights a week and then it was off to the pub. Rugby tours particularly to Wales took on a legendary status. The golden rule being 'what went on in tours stayed on tour', in other words no snitching about what went on off the pitch. Rugby union was still considered to be a game of 'the toffs' and certainly much of its strength came from old boys' clubs often putting out six or seven teams each Saturday. This was made possible because so many young men acquired jobs close to where they had been to school. Further north there was an even tougher form of the game and played professionally.

The game of rugby league dates back to late Victorian England. Again even in sport class differences were accentuated. Injuries and tours away from home meant a loss of income for working class players. So in the 1890s the northern union broke away from the RFU and for decades there was no meeting point between the two codes. The amateurs may have sneered but a new game was born. Rules were changed as well with the players on each team being reduced from fifteen to thirteen. This had the effect of speeding the game up which now required a higher degree of fitness. A league was formed so each match had a result that mattered. Fierce rivalries between neighbouring towns were established and large crowds for the games became a regular backdrop to northern weekends. A young Gerry Southworth remembers going to see Wakefield Trinity in 1946. All the matches teetered on the edge of outright violence but were skilful also. This was a game for real men, not those posh southern softies. All the matches were partisan but Gerry recalls it was Wakefield's games against Leeds that raised the blood pressure most.

At the other end of the spectrum was the gentle game of tennis. At least as it was played by most in the 1940s. Although many public parks usually had a couple of hard courts for hire, tennis clubs struck a more elitist pose. Youngsters looked on as their older brother or sister struck up their first romantic interest. Middle class parents thought a tennis club was a place where their children could meet others from a similar background. On a bright summer's afternoon it was all tea cake and Lloyd Loom chairs to a background of polite pat-a-cake tennis. That of course only applied to mixed doubles where it was considered extremely rude for a chap to serve too fast or crunch a volley at a young lady on the other side of the net. Where young boys or their older brothers were concerned all bets were off as they sought to overpower each other, red faced and sweaty as they tried to impress those watching from the clubhouse.

Tennis in those far off days was played with wooden racquets which had to be kept in a press when not in use. Equipment for all of the sports youngsters played some eighty years ago was often very different from its modern counterpart. Tennis shoes were called plimsolls rather than trainers. They cost just a few shillings before the marketing gurus persuaded people to pay hundreds of pounds for the modern equivalent. Football boots were also sturdy and tough. Made from leather they laced up to the ankle and were supplemented by bulky shin pads worn under woollen socks. Soccer was a rough physical contact sport. Crunching tackles and shoulder barging were allowed even on the goalkeeper. Often played on muddy pitches where it was difficult to shift the ball more than a few metres, physicality rather than skill typified the British game which was increasingly exposed in international matches. Early memories of playing cricket conjure thoughts as a youngster of going out to bat with pads so large that it was impossible to run at more than a trot.

Talking of trotting, horses were the obsession of many young girls particularly those living in the countryside. To own a horse or pony was just a dream for most youngsters but there were stables where in return for mucking out it was possible to get an occasional ride. Lessons were also available and the best birthday present possible for some was a course of lessons at the local riding school. There were regular gymkhanas to attend and pony club camps. Show jumping surged in popularity after the London Olympics when an early role model emerged in Pat Smythe. She was invited to join the English team in 1947 in a sport formally reckoned to be too dangerous for women to compete in. Pat Smythe went onto enjoy incredible international success boosted in the 1950s by the popularity of televising the International Horse Show from White City.

Pat Smythe was able to show young girls that it was not necessary to come from a monied background to succeed. As in other sports it was more a matter of hard work combined with a natural talent that normally won through. 1949 saw another equine sport emerge where it certainly helped to have wealthy parents but did not exclude natural talent. Three-day eventing was staged in the grand surroundings of Badminton Park. It tested the horse and rider to display a range of skills. The first day was devoted to dressage to be followed on day two by a formidable cross-country course. Here horse and rider encountered a range of formidable obstacles to overcome. The final day (providing the horse passed the vet's inspection) was to tackle a stiff show-jumping course. The idea was to test the skill of both horse and rider. From these early beginnings the sport has flourished, usually taking place in very grand surroundings and becoming a social as well as a major sporting event.

Sport formed an important part of a youngster's upbringing and even for those who hated it there was no easy way to escape. For the enthusiasts it formed a memorable background to our formative years, whether being actively involved or just watching. Sport was reckoned to be character forming. Ideally you were encouraged to be a good loser and gracious in victory whilst encouraging support of the underdog. Obviously this was not always the case but overall it was an ethos that stuck.

Strangely of all the memories of sporting Britain in the 1940s it is not the feats of the stars or even of our own limited successes, rather it is the voices of those broadcasters who were keeping us informed. Harold Abrahams the voice of athletics, or excitable Raymond Glendenning? But no, surely it has to be the voices of cricket. Sitting next to a bakelite wireless set listening to the gentle Hampshire burr of John Arlott to be followed by the plummy tones of E.W. Swanton summing up the day's play. Happy days, unforgettable memories.

Chapter 24

Youngsters After the War

After all the excitement of Victory Parades and street parties, the expectations of children was high. Certainly adults appeared more relaxed and it was good not having to troop to the basement at school as the the air warning system wailed away, but generally life was much the same. Still rationing, power cuts, any sense of euphoria gone.

At school a raft of returning teachers arrived having recently been demobbed. Most had become used to women teachers, many of them young, attractive and approachable only to be replaced by often bad tempered and strict masters. Boys particularly were picked out for bad behaviour and slovenly dress. These men were bringing back a touch of military discipline to school life. 'Stand up straight boy', they were ordered and 'straighten that tie, you look a mess lad'. Why did they all seem so bad tempered we wondered, but of course none of us knew what had happened to them during the war and despite our requests they were not about to tell us.

For years children had been allowed to leave school at fourteen and many could not wait. Some parents also were keen for their kids to add to the family income and so when in 1944 the leaving age was extended to fifteen there were many gloomy faces, and behaviour in the last year of those wanting to leave worsened and truancy increased. For those wanting to further their education there was a raft of exams to be taken. Passing the eleven-plus exam was considered by many parents as a pathway to success for their children allowing them the opportunity to attend a grammar or similar school. Pressure was put on many youngsters and the results awaited with baited breath. Obviously if a child failed it did not consign them to a life without chances or one who passed to a guilded future, but the exam was an important juncture in many youngsters' lives. Next came a period of swotting for the dreaded school certificate exams and for the brightest, matriculation. Obtaining these qualifications certainly opened up enhanced job prospects. Many looked on as their siblings entered the type of employment that their parents would never have dreamt of.

Without doubt those left in the elementary and village schools were seldom encouraged to be ambitious. There appeared to be a presumption that they would take factory or agricultural jobs depending on either a city or country location. Of course there were many who subsequently bucked the system and went on to huge success but it was a fight not to be consigned to the type of employment seemingly designated for you.

It was sport that allowed some from deprived backgrounds to break free. There was fame on offer if you were brilliant at cricket or football, but no great riches (how different from today). Boxing was probably the best way for a young man from the slums to make a fortune. Of course many tried this route only to find themselves consigned to fight in small halls and being paid just a few pounds to get regularly smashed, often with long term health effects. For those few who did reach the top there were dodgy managers and promoters to deal with. A much repeated theme is of a champion losing all the money he has made and ending up sad and destitute.

No matter, the magic of sport had an almost hypnotic attraction for many youngsters for both playing and watching. Maybe suffering a few bruises or even broken limbs was a risk worth taking in order to compete, but surely attending a big match was safe. Unfortunately on a damp February day in 1946 an unbelievable series of events led to a tragedy largely forgotten today.

Burnden Park, home to Bolton Wanderers, was like most first class grounds at the time where the vast majority of the crowd stood to watch the match on windswept terraces. As the match progressed people pushed and strained to get a better view partially contained by metal crush barriers. Stewards had been unable to restrict those desperate to get into the ground and there were many gatecrashers. It was later estimated that an astonishing eighty five thousand were in the ground, way over the safe limits. Part of the ground had been requisitioned by the government during the war and was not in use, further reducing the safe capacity. In those days tickets were purchased at the turnstiles rather than in advance, causing a huge backlog of fans trying to gain entry. Already worried the authorities decided to close the turnstiles twenty minutes before kick-off. Fans started climbing over walls and due to the crush outside a locked gate was opened letting even more fans to charge in. Still they came pushing and shoving with fans eventually spilling onto the side of the pitch.

The game started on schedule but soon pressure from behind saw fans being forced onto the pitch. At this point the game was stopped as spectators were pushed back into the crowd. Shortly afterwards two crush barriers collapsed. Some lost their balance and were crushed by the uncontrollable surge of the spectators standing behind them. Once again the game was halted and the police informed the referee of the likelihood of fatalities. At this point the players left the pitch. Astonishingly some of the dead were just covered with coats and laid out along the touchline. After an interval the game was resumed. There was no break at half time as the teams just changed ends. Ironically it was a dull game ending in a goal-less draw. The decision not to abandon the game was bizarre and sickened the players when they were able to understand what had really happened, although many attending the match that day had no idea that anyone had been killed. Sadly thirty three people died that afternoon with hundreds including children injured. A subsequent inquiry led to a tightening of safety regulations at grounds, but crowd disasters at football matches continued to haunt 'the beautiful game' for decades to come.

On a lighter note youngsters at that time were presented with a new hero. In October 1946 Dick Barton Special Agent was broadcast each weekday night at six forty-five in the evening. At the sound of the show's exciting signature tune the 'Devil's Gallop' being played, youngsters, particularly the boys, were glued to their wireless sets. Dick Barton, supported by his sidekicks Jock and Snowy, conspired to defeat all kinds of despicable enemies normally portrayed as foreigners with funny accents. The dangers the three encountered became ever more outlandish, but none of us cared. Each night presented even more bizarre dangers, and each episode ended on a cliffhanger with poor old Dick surely destined to die. In fact he survived for five years until 1951 with the main part being played by a variety of actors. Radio increasingly became an important part of children's lives with a far more popular schedule available particularly on the Light Programme.

A glance through a copy of Radio Times at the beginning of 1947 emphasised how listening to the wireless was now a major source of entertainment across all age groups. All tastes were catered for with the addition of the Third Programme in 1946. This provided the main source for serious classical music supplemented by talks and lectures aimed at a minority audience. The Home Service had widened its scope but was still the main source of news and religious output. There were also ambitious dramas and plays often featuring well known actors and actresses. Long running favourites like 'Any Questions' were also establishing themselves. Outside sporting events were also included with Rex Alston commentating on the second half of the rugby international between France and Ireland from Stade Colombes in Paris.

Saturday night saw 'auntie' loosening her stays with the favourite 'In Town Tonight' starting at 7.45 in the evening. Leading celebrities staying in the capital were interviewed whilst Brian Johnston was undertaking a series of stunts in a part of the show called 'Let's Go Somewhere'. Then at eight o'clock 'Music Hall' starring Max Bygraves and a full supporting cast ran for an hour.

But while the Home Service now offered a wide range of entertainment it was the Light Programme that most appealed to youngsters. Even the under fives were catered for with 'Listen With Mother'. This was a programme of nursery rhymes, stories and music. It was whilst lying ill in bed that youngsters realised how much their mothers relied on the radio. Often it remained switched on all day. Feeling ill with one of the common children's illnesses, it was comforting to hear the radio in the background. For many the day started with 'Housewives Choice', a record request programme hosted by Robert McDermot. The BBC's obsession with theatre organ music persisted. No, not Sandy MacPherson but music played by Andrew Fenner being relayed from the Gaumont in Kilburn. 'Music While You Work' lived on whilst the enduring radio soap 'Mrs. Dale's Diary' started at mid-day. With relatively few women working in 1947 they were further catered for each afternoon with 'Woman's Hour' although they did not cover the racy subjects that are aired today. Rather safe subjects like 'Flowers In The House' or a talk on stately homes was as controversial as the programme strayed. Over on the Home Service 'Children's Hour' continued to flourish.

Although the fledgling television service had now started transmitting it was to the radio that people of all ages still turned to for their entertainment. The scope of programmes by the end of the decade was impressive, with increasing live outside coverage of state and sporting occasions. Iconic shows like 'Desert Island Discs' and 'Any Questions' remain relevant today as does 'The Archers' which was first broadcast in 1950, and despite the arrival of television and other forms of direct access entertainment the popularity of steam radio persists.

Whereas Hollywood and Disney still dominated the film industry, youngsters were able to see that during the war years that British film makers were fighting back with a series of comedies. Their 'U' classification meant that a film was suitable for children aged four and over and could be watched by children unaccompanied. The first Ealing comedy was 'Hue And Cry' starring Alastair Sim and set against a backdrop of war damaged London. The storyline was pretty weak and the film received a mixed reception. Within a couple of years the studio had hit its straps with the hugely popular 'Passport To Pimlico' with Margaret Rutherford and 'Whisky Galore' starring the husky voiced Joan Greenwood.

At the beginning of 1947 many remember going to see 'Great Expectations'. Based on the novel by Charles Dickens it was directed by David Lean who went on to achieve international acclaim with films like 'Lawrence Of Arabia' and 'Bridge On The River Kwai'. My father took me to see 'The Third Man'. I was about ten at the time and though I have vague memories of Orson Welles and Joseph Cotton meeting to a sinister backdrop of a gloomy Vienna, it is the evocative zither music that still haunts. This was a time of record cinema attendances with over one and a half million tickets bought during 1946. Another predictable boost was due to the boom in births as these new born babies joined the ranks of children of the 1940s.

Going to the pictures was sheer escapism for children and youngsters from a drab and bleak world awaiting them outside. For young boys it was the tales of adventure or comedies being played out on screen that enthralled them most. Their sisters were drawn more by films involving animals and, as they entered their teens, of love and romance. For some girls visits to the cinema were influential in their choice of career.

Many girls attended dancing classes. These were often confined to ballet but this was far too constricting for three youngsters, two of whom became professional dancers. Sylvia Cooney and Iris Chapple both loved the spectacular films of Fred Astaire and Ginger Rogers. They could imagine themselves descending the sweeping staircase as the chorus parted for them to take centre stage. Jean Sporle was younger and would have to wait her turn but she also saw her future on the stage.

Of course many of those who were children at the outbreak of war were now ready to take their first faltering steps into the world of employment. Sylvia Cooney could not wait and as soon as she celebrated her fifteenth birthday she was off. Still a stunning looking woman in old age she remembers that for her the bright lights beckoned. Her good looks were obviously going to help but since taking tap dancing lessons from the age of eleven she had felt fit to take the world by storm. An extrovert and a born performer and accompanied by an accordion she had the confidence to entertain the crowds taking shelter in the underground during the blitz. With the confidence of youth she joined her older sister and a close friend to form the Alpine Trio. Travelling the country and living out of a suitcase whilst having to deal with grumpy landladies was not the glamorous life she had imagined.

After seeing an advertisement in The Stage she went for an audition at the Windmill Theatre without telling her parents. At her audition Vivian Van Damm needed little time to realise that she was a perfect addition to his company. She was young, beautiful and a great dancer with a natural poise and deportment. His assistant, a real martinet, was not so impressed as she really put Sylvia through her paces prior to her appearing in her first show.

It was her father rather than her mother who was horrified. He went to see Van Damm who calmed his fears and issued him with free tickets to see the show. This slightly placated him for although there was some nudity on stage everything was not only tasteful but professionally produced. Sylvia spent two happy years at the theatre. Much to her increasing shame her father insisted on picking her up from the stage door each night. During her time at the Windmill she had always been in the chorus, never appearing in the nude. With pressure now being put on her she decided reluctantly to resign. She had loved the experience and the excitement and made many friends but it was time to move on. She went on to appear at a number of West End clubs including the Cafe Anglaise. Then like so many before and after her she fell in love and married, denying us the chance that she may well have become a true star.

Fashion is also something of an obsession for many young girls. The war years and the austerity that followed required great ingenuity to make any impression. It was a decade of make do and mend. Now there was hope albeit arriving via Paris. The editor of Vogue enthused: 'round hipline, small shoulder, pulled in waist, longer skirt.' She goes on to describe: 'the skirt maybe full petal-shaped or spreading with unpressed pleats. It maybe straight, but either way it descends to anything from fourteen to eight inches from the ground.' The New Look had arrived. The public, particularly the young loved it. Grumpy lumpy old Labour MP Bessie Braddock hated it. She did not approve of the longer skirt. Surely a waste of material and suggested that British women should be happy with the clothes they already had. Some hope. It was six months until the new style appeared in British stores but with clothes still rationed it was time to fish out the old Singer sewing machine as young teenage girls encouraged their mothers to brush up on their dressmaking skills. For Jean Sporle the outfit was not complete unless she was carrying an elegant fastened umbrella.

So the New Look was the first faltering step into the bright sunlight of a new post war Britain. But hang on, not so fast. Rationing still had the country in its cloying embrace. Perhaps their mums and elder sisters were going to look smarter, but youngsters craved more and tastier food. In 1947 the pollster Gallup invited people to list their perfect meal for a special occasion. Surely the result would have raised a superior smug smile on any self-respecting French housewife. The choice for this epic blow-out was fairly predictable.

Tomato soup was to be followed by sole (no indication on how this was to be cooked was noted). After a short pause it was time for roast chicken, potatoes, peas and, surprisingly, Brussels sprouts. The choice of pudding was trifle and cream followed by cheese and biscuits. All this to be washed down with a schooner of sherry. Sweet, no doubt. Well it is always good to dream but food rationing had become even more draconian. You were now allowed one ounce of bacon per week, three pounds of potatoes, two ounces of butter plus three ounces of margarine. Just a single ounce of cooking fat plus a miserable two ounces of cheese. Meat eaters were entitled to one shilling's worth. Half a pound of bread a day was permitted with a pound of jam or marmalade for those with a sweet tooth. Only the likes of 'Chips' Channon and his aristocratic chums could afford to eat out and they were not happy either. James Lees-Milne moaned: 'the food in England is worse than during the war, dry and tasteless even at Brook's.' Tinned snoek at two and nine pence did not hit the spot either. Did we really win the war, moaned our parents. Better times must be coming though and there was even talk of some of us going off to enjoy our first holiday at the seaside.

As a child much of importance passes you by. Later in life we began to take flying off for our holiday for granted. Until the end of the war aeroplanes were generally to be feared as they ducked and dived above us, but at the end of May 1946 London airport re-opened for civilian flights. Unrecognisable from today's major hub, it continued to be known as London airport until being renamed Heathrow in 1966. For most youngsters it was going to be many years before they took to the sky, and it was only much later in life that we began to take flying off on holiday for granted.

For the time being children's lives carried on much as before. We played the same games and read the same comics. Enid Blyton continued to churn out endless books including the introduction of 'Noddy and Big Ears'. As we continued to grow we endured squeezing our feet into shoes that no longer fitted because we had no spare coupons. A further nod to things to come saw Tommy Lawton transferred from Chelsea to Notts County for the then eye watering sum of twenty thousand pounds. We all, both adults and children, strained trying to detect the better future we had all been promised. Little sign of it yet, but don't forget we have been promised our first real holiday.

Chapter 25

Sea Air and Candy Floss

During the war those of us who lived in inland towns and cities dreamt of our first seaside holiday. Would it really live up to our expectations? We would have seen photographs of our parents standing self consciously on some promenade with the sea in the background. The black and white photographs make everything look rather gloomy. It was copies of pre-war magazines advertising towns like Blackpool or Eastbourne that fascinated me. In these the sun was always shining and young ladies in swimming costumes smiled a welcome from across the years. Most of us could scarcely wait, but wait we had to. In 1946 most of the beaches were either mined or covered in rolls of barbed wire.

After the savage winter of the following year summer came early with a heat-wave that started at the end of May and extended well into June. This was enough. It was as if a starting gun had been sounded. Main-line railway stations were invaded by a huge army of holiday makers and day trippers. For those who had not been evacuated and had never been on a train the adventure was about to begin. Stations crowded with passengers seeking the correct platform, porters dragging trolleys laden with bags and trunks, and the vast rather frightening steam engine wheezing and grunting as if anxious to leave. It was easy to get lost amongst the scrum of people. Tension was high as luggage was heaved up onto racks. The piercing whistle and the carriages shuddering as if drawing their first breath as the holiday was about to begin.

It was the expansion of the railways in Victorian Britain that led to small towns and villages being developed into seaside attractions. Sea air had long been thought to aid good health. Now suddenly droves of working class communities were able to enjoy the thrill of the seaside. Coastal towns vied with each other to lay on added attractions for their visitors and the unique British seaside holiday mushroomed. Grand hotels were built some with turrets rather like castles providing protection from the hoi polloi clogging up the elegant promenades. One hundred years later the segregation remained as post-war Britain took to the beaches.

My first seaside visit was to Margate. It was in 1947 and the heat-wave continued. The overall impression was of boisterous crowds milling around not quite sure where they were going or what to do. The people were mostly from London, rowdy and friendly. Only the young girls were dressed suitably in the burning heat. Their dads and boyfriends continued to wear thick trousers and boots. Some had taken off their shirts and paraded proudly in thick vests with knotted handkerchiefs protecting their heads. Fat ladies squealed as lifting their skirts they paddled in the sea, running up the beach as a big wave caught them unawares. Old men, fag in mouth, sat stoically in deck chairs still wearing their Sunday best suit. Back on the promenade photographers tried to drum up some trade. I remember there was a man with a chained monkey sitting on his shoulder whilst he played the accordion. With sweet rationing still firmly in place I tried to get my dad to buy me a toffee apple which looked so inviting. I had to settle for candy floss which also looked inviting but was a disappointment.

For many their first holiday was not taken in a grand hotel but rather a boarding house. These obviously varied alarmingly in the comfort and the food they provided. Many served breakfast and then the guests were in effect banned from the house until tea or the evening meal was served. This was tolerable during good weather but the sight of wet bedraggled holiday makers taking shelter from the rain lingers on. It was also expensive for parents trying to keep their children amused. It was not unusual that an eagerly awaited holiday could turn into a nightmare if the rain continued. Tempers frayed, parents argued and children whined.

Most seaside towns offered a huge variety of entertainments. Leading seaside towns had wooden Victorian piers jutting far out into the sea. Paying for entry at the turnstile you could walk above the crashing waves. Along the way vendors sold ice creams and kiss-me-quick hats. There was live music too coming from the bandstand at the end of the pier. Stallholders sold saucy postcards for you to send to friends and family. There was generally a cafe where a welcome cup of tea and a cake was on offer and a bottle of Tizer for the kids. People hovered outside a small tent. Inside it was possible to make out a sallow-skinned woman. Sitting on a table in front of her was a crystal ball mounted on a wooden stand.

'Tell your fortune?' she enquired holding up tarot cards. A young woman enters and the curtains are drawn but people stand close by eavesdropping. Concert parties were another attraction but everything cost money and for most spending had to be carefully monitored to avoid running out before it was time to go home.

During good weather the beach was the biggest draw. Having paid for the hire of your deckchairs it was time to claim your few feet of space. As the tide went out the children made sand castles. A bucket, spade and sand is all most young children need for hours of entertainment. From Blackpool to Southend and Scarborough to Weston Super Mare all resorts offered a variety of attractions. Popular amongst them were traditional Punch and Judy shows, now much watered down. Certainly back eighty years ago the shows were really violent and seemingly we all loved them, shouting out our warnings or encouragement. We were an unsophisticated audience, both parents and children just seeking enjoyment wherever we could find it after all the hardships of the war years. Pleasures as simple as riding a bike. Arthur Price Jones had always coveted having a bicycle to ride but on his first holiday in Rhyl this had still not been forthcoming. On the front at Rhyl (known as Thrillsville) was what he described as a pit where it was possible to hire a bike. Not to take out to explore the surrounding countryside, rather just riding around in a circle watched on by his parents. To us viewing this today it seems really sad but to the young lad it was a great and still remembered thrill. Such small pleasures were important to a generation generally deprived of tiny enjoyments that would surely go unnoticed today.

For children one of the main attractions at the seaside was the donkey rides. We would stand in line waiting to be seated astride what would hopefully be our favourite. For inner city kids a donkey was as close as they were likely to get to riding a proper horse but none the less leaving a memory that endured. Jean Sporle's parents took her each year to Clacton-on-Sea for their annual holiday. It was a popular resort for Londoners who really knew how to let their hair down and enjoy this break from their work. She remembers the donkeys being led down from West Avenue each morning accompanied by a small army of willing helpers. Another highlight of their holiday was a trip to the West Cliff Theatre.

Almost all of the seaside resorts had a theatre or music hall and well known stars would be booked for the summer season. Major destinations like Blackpool or Brighton offering the biggest stars to help tempt the punters in. 1947 was probably not a vintage year for the West Cliff Theatre with their headline act staring the now largely forgotten Nosmo King. One of the supporting acts was a recently demobbed Frankie Howerd experiencing his first summer season. These summer shows allowed many future stars to learn their trade. It was a tough training as the tradition of giving 'the bird' to acts that did not engage their audience persisted from the Victorian Music Hall.

Tradition continued to play a key role in the post war holiday experience. Wakes Week saw whole towns close down as they made off to the sea. The Lancashire cotton towns headed for Blackpool and other north western resorts whilst the hosiery workers from Leicester traditionally headed for Skegness. These mass local shutdowns stemmed from the time when workers began to have paid holidays, but the origin of Wakes dates back to medieval times when villages had a holiday and feast with a dedication to their local parish church. Many of the saints associated with parish churches celebrate their feast days in the summer extending the link with Wakes holidays.

Additional entertainment for demanding holiday makers came in the form of fairgrounds which were normally found either on or close to the seafront. Fun fairs were originally started by gypsies and now formed an important part of the traditional seaside holiday. It was a good way for children to learn the value of money and how to budget. Given a set amount they had to work out what attraction they could afford. The trouble was that the choice was bewildering and few could afford to choose all the rides. Children like me tended to rush in and spend their pocket money quickly before regretting it as newly made friends spent theirs more carefully.

One of the cheapest attractions was a swing boat. Two of you sat opposite each other pulling on ropes to get the wooden boat swinging higher and higher. The pleasure beach at Blackpool offered all the latest rides as well as traditional old favourites. Boys of course loved the dodgem cars although the real fun was had by bashing into as many others as possible navigating the rink. For those wanting to be both exhilarated and frightened the big dipper was the answer. This combination of terror and yet knowing you were really safe was irresistible. For young children a ride on a helter-skelter was thrilling enough. Nervously climbing to the top you then sat on a mat before descending down the spiral to be welcomed by your mum. Not frightened anymore, you now inevitably wanted another go. Perhaps the most popular ride of all was the roundabout which had the attraction of horses again. Hanging on tightly, the world spun beneath you to a background of hurdy gurdy music.

Still there were more rides to try like the Ferris wheel and those with water hazards. For teenagers there was always the tunnel of love or alternatively the spooky ghost train where hopefully your young lady would need a comforting kiss and cuddle. All the fun of the fair on offer within a short space typified the attraction of a traditional British holiday. Simple unsophisticated fun but it was a model soon to come under threat from cheap foreign holidays

There was one final attraction. The circus under the big top would often pitch their tents at a seaside resort. They drew in full houses particularly when the weather was bad. Doubtless these shows would be considered cruel today but they certainly had the power to thrill. Audiences gasped at the skill and daring of the high wire acts and laughed at the antics of the clowns, except the sad faced white clown with tears rolling down his face. Everyone loved the bare-backed riders and the elegant elephants performing their tricks. The finale was often left to the lion tamer. To sit so close to these wild animals controlled by a single man with a whip did strike me, even as a boy, as being cruel, but youngsters don't dwell on things, as there is always more excitement waiting round the next corner. Even before the foreign holiday took hold there was one man who spotted an opportunity to extend and refine the British summer holiday. His name was Billy Butlin.

Billy Butlin was born in Cape Town and spent time in Canada before arriving in Great Britain in 1921 whilst still in his early twenties. He secured a job in the family fairground trade initially painting and refitting rides, but it did not take him long to set up his first hoopla stall which quickly showed him a profit. This set his entrepreneurial juices flowing but the fairground was a very tough and sometimes violent place to work. Billy soon learnt how to look after himself and it was rumoured that he always carried a knife. He painted his expanding number of stalls in bright blue and yellow, a colour combination that he used years later in his first holiday camp.

His expansion continued when he negotiated a deal with Bertram Mills circus securing the best pitches for his stalls close to the entrance. Always restless he now wanted to cash in on the seaside holiday trade. He settled on a stretch of sand dunes in Skegness which he leased from the estate of Lord Scarborough. Unable to afford the clearing of the site to make it suitable for his stalls he hit on the idea of selling the sand to local builders providing they filled their own lorries to take it away. He then set up four hoopla stalls, soon adding a helter-skelter and a haunted house. The punters flooded in and next he added a scenic railway. To overcome the seasonal nature of his business he started renting old factories and garages and turned them into amusement arcades that could stay open all year. He was the first to import dodgem cars and he secured sole European distribution. Soon they were appearing not only at Skegness but other prime locations in Rhyl, Clacton and Felixstowe. It was during this period that the idea of holiday camps niggled away. He watched hordes of holiday makers roaming around with time on their hands, money to spend but nowhere to go. Not far from his Skegness base he realised that the village of Mablethorpe with its acres of agricultural land overlooking the sea would surely be an ideal site for Britain's first holiday camp.

An advertisement in the Daily Express drew a phenomenal response. Who could resist a holiday that included three meals a day and free entertainment for between thirty five shillings and three pounds a week depending on the time of year. The food was terrible, the service awful but Butlin had hit on a goldmine of an idea. By the outbreak of war camps were also opened at Clacton and another under construction at Filey. All the sites were requisitioned during the war and Butlin used this time to buy up all the fairground equipment he could find as their value had slumped to almost zero. Thus by 1946 he was in a position to realise his dream.

By 1947 Butlin had added three new camps in Filey, Ayr and Pwllheli. He had hit on a winning formula for a British public long denied much fun. The camps were huge, offering accommodation mainly in pretty basic chalets, but few people appeared to care when they had the prospect of a week or even a fortnight of relaxation and entertainment.

Each camp offered a ballroom, an assortment of bars and a sports hall where snooker and table tennis was on offer. There was a putting green or crazy golf. There was always something to do from morning to night. Campers were divided into different teams or houses so there were constant competitions from tug of war to beauty contests, including the ever popular 'glamorous granny'. Each site was situated right by the sea but there were also huge swimming pools which still became packed during fine weather. Campers sat in deck chairs watching the show-offs doing somersaults from the high diving board.

The appeal of the camps was that they suited all ages. Parents with young children knew their kids were safe within the confines of the camp and therefore they were free to relax and enjoy themselves. For the children each day was filled with competitions and organised fun. Whilst they entered a fancy dress competition their fathers were busy trying to win the knobbly knees competition. There were of course complaints, some comparing the complexes to concentration camps. Teenagers loved the camps, particularly if they were able to go with friends rather than parents. It did not take long for misgivings to be voiced about the sexual freedom the camps provided for youngsters away from the prying eyes of their parents. The outrage of the elderly only encouraged more teenagers to persuade their parents that it was time for them to fly the nest, at least for a few days.

Certainly there were many breathless holiday romances. The Redcoats who organised the entertainment at the camps were often being targeted by those wanting to throw off the conventions of the day. Before the advent of the pill the risk of pregnancy still cooled the ardour of all but the most determined. So there it was, something for everyone and the bookings for the camps continued to boom.

It is interesting to get the thoughts of a female contributor to mass observation who visited Butlin's camp in Filey in 1947. She reported that because it was late in the season the camp was only half full. Astonishingly the camp still had some five thousand guests. The three meals served each day offered no choice and meant having to sit at the same table with fellow guests that they may not really like. A highlight on Saturday night was 'Butlin follies of 1947'. It was a variety show starring many of the resident Redcoats. She reports that the audience packed into the theatre: 'were most appreciative applauding each turn vociferously'. Next morning she was wakened by reveille blasted out on a tannoy system. Each day's programme had at least one contest and on Sunday it was 'holiday lovelies'. Over the next few days she appears to have generally enjoyed camp life, particularly the formal dances.

All good and original ideas are generally copied and Butlin was not the only camp provider. Fred Pontin's camps were smaller and cheaper. Although not offering the range of attractions, Pontin also found a huge and lucrative market. He even copied the Redcoat idea, calling his entertainers Bluecoats. Warners also entered the market but it is Butlin's that is still remembered. The British seaside experience although varied was unique in the 1940s. From grand hotels to dingy boarding houses and bawdy holiday camps, the public's expectations were low. With that established there was a bottled up desire for enjoyment, even if by today's standards what was on offer was pretty grim. Those years were the first stumble into the package holiday world that was soon to migrate to the beaches of the Costa Brava and moans about terrible food and 'Spanish tummy'. Sir Billy Butlin (as he was later to become) pocketed his millions and the travel market moved on.

For some young men their first ever two week holiday was to be followed by two years service in the armed forces. It added a certain desperation to enjoy themselves.

Chapter 26

Get Fell In

Thousands of boys who were children at the start of the decade found themselves liable for military service by its end. With so many commitments across the world Britain needed to replace those who had served during the war and were now awaiting demob. Conscription for young men aged eighteen was introduced, although national service as it became known was not fully introduced until 1949.

Not long after a young man's eighteenth birthday a dreaded buff envelope dropped through their letterbox. This instructed them to attend a local government office. Here they underwent a medical examination followed by a written test. The medical was based on eyesight, hearing and physical capacity. This combined with the written test gave an indication of the conscript's potential and the type of posting he was best suited to. At this stage the young man was asked which branch of the service he favoured although the majority were normally consigned to the army. High born recruits and those who had attended major public schools were considered for the Royal Navy or one of the more pukka army outfits. Previous family connections were also important. Historically the Royal Air Force was the least snobbish of the armed forces and they tended to welcome intelligent grammar school entrants. Initially recruits were required to serve for eighteen months but this was quickly increased to two years.

Based on the written results men were placed into different categories. They ranged from those able to assimilate instructions and act on their own initiative to those who would require constant supervision. These recruits were designated the status of dull, a category which was subsequently refined to dull and definitely dull. Dull they may have been but this did not stop them or the brighter recruits seeking reasons why they considered themselves unfit for service. Some simply did not turn up for their medical and written test, most of these were often quickly tracked down but a few (reckoned to be under one percent) just vanished. The medics were confronted with all types of wheezes. Pretending to be really stupid was the most common but this rarely washed with the authorities. A few were so desperate that they attempted to pierce their eardrum with a knitting needle. Perhaps the best bet was to appear covered in cologne and generally mince around. A more subtle approach was to wear your sister's or mother's underwear. Until recently homosexuals were banned from serving in the armed forces.

After a lull of a few weeks call-up papers arrived and armed with travel documents it was off to the nearest mainline railway station and then onwards to the unit they had been assigned to. Here for possibly the first time in their lives young men from across the social divide were crammed together. It was a revelation for all concerned. Titled toffs sleeping in the next bed to a labourer, or a young man educated at Marlborough or Rugby cheek by jowl with dockers or young men who had already 'done time' in prison. Strangely, normally it was the public schoolboys who settled in best. Many thought the living conditions were better than their school dormitories and the grub tastier and more plentiful. Many working class lads had never left home and certainly some really struggled.

The army particularly quickly tried to eliminate any sparks of individuality. Basic training was designed to get young men to obey orders without question, no matter how seemingly unreasonable or stupid. The first step was a military haircut. Carefully coiffured locks were shorn away. Brylcreemed smoothies reduced to a short back and sides. Suitably depressed by the turn of events it was now time to collect your gear. Uniforms that roughly fitted were issued by the quartermaster and his assistants. Also pairs of 'jungle greens', underwear and of course the all important pair of boots. The next days when square bashing had finished for the day it was time to polish those boots. First the pimples had to be removed from the toecaps courtesy of a heated spoon.

Bedding was also issued on the first day and learning to make the bed ready for daily inspection became routine, although stripped and thrown to the floor if it did not meet with the approval of the bellowing NCO. The first night spent with strangers in crowded barracks was too much for some who cried themselves to sleep, but most were so exhausted they just crashed out. Basic training continued with endless hours of square bashing. Each platoon was overseen by a sergeant and a couple of NCOs. There were usually up to eight platoons with each intake and the pressure to be awarded top platoon on completion of basic training was fierce, prompted by sizeable bets being placed by those in charge. A weekend off was given when various inoculations were pumped into arms. Some people had a very strong reaction and took to their beds whilst their mates without side effects headed for the NAAFI. Fit again it was time to take on the assault course followed by a forced march. Map reading skills would be tested by dumping pairs of recruits miles from anywhere and expecting them to get back to base in the shortest possible time. By now the recruits were fitter than when they joined and even beginning to enjoy life.

Basic training normally ran for about eight weeks during which there would gradually be less shouting while the training got easier. Lectures and graphic films were shown of the dangers of VD. This certainly cooled young men's ardour for a moment, but as they had no chance of meeting the opposite sex all of this was forgotten by the time these would-be gigolos were back in circulation. Now it was time for a spot of indoctrination. The history and the pride you should feel for the regiment, squadron or ship that you were attached to. To the surprise of many there was now a genuine pride in their unit and the fellow servicemen that they had lived so close to over the recent weeks. Of course there were disputes, even serious fights and assaults, but generally looking back on their basic training most felt they had benefitted from the experience. There is a story of a titled recruit gaining massive street cred by composing love letters for others to copy and send home to girlfriends. Astonished that the boy who had previously been totally unromantic could put his feeling for her in words apparently worked wonders (if only in the short term).

At the end of basic training was the passing out parade. By now the recruits had learned how to handle, strip and clean an ancient 303 rifle and a Bren gun. He was fitter, smarter and was ready for his first home leave. The sergeant who had previously screamed, shouted and abused suddenly seemed human after all particularly if his platoon had done well in the parade. He was even likely to share a few drinks with his lads before they moved on and he welcomed the next batch of callow unsuspecting recruits. Travelling home in uniform was a proud experience for most. Public transport was full of military personnel but the walk up the street you grew up in with your kit bag hoisted on your shoulder is a memory many later fondly referred to. Now where? Some craved a foreign posting, although preferably not Palestine as that was really dangerous. Cyprus perhaps or Hong Kong. Many wanted a home posting but it was out of their hands as you had to go where you were sent. For some this meant excitement and danger but for most it was months of boredom with seemingly nothing of importance to do. Making up jobs in an attempt to look busy, enduring endless days and fostering a growing sense of resentment.

Brian Abbott grew up in Penge in south London. Attending the local grammar school he fitted the profile required by the Royal Air Force. After his basic training he imagined and hoped for a posting in the far east. Instead he spent most of the next two years in various RAF camps in Germany being under-employed. Perhaps the best way to get the most out of national service was to apply for a commission. What was required other than a posh school and a relative who had served previously.

The attrition rate during the war led to many being commissioned who normally would have remained in the ranks. The sniffy regiments referred to these men 'as officers but not gentlemen' and in post war conscription old prejudices still held sway once more. Snobbery and class divide invaded every aspect of life.

Whilst all three services did commission conscripts it was extremely rare in the Navy. Because of this public schools steered their pupils towards the Army or RAF. The Navy demanded academic distinction, or at least a background in engineering combined with a privileged upbringing which ruled most recruits out of contention. The RAF were the least impressed by background. They continued to recruit mainly from bright grammar school boys or those from lesser public schools. It was generally accepted that getting a commission in the Air Force was more difficult than in the Army. Some still opted for the Air Force, even if it meant serving in the ranks.

So it was that most national service officers were to be found in the Army. Many public school pupils had joined the Combined Cadet Force (CCF) which gave them a basic understanding of service life. During their basic training recruits were interviewed by a personal selection officer who attempted to identify potential officer material. At this stage it was educational ability that was important, but so was the school you attended and your family background. For a time potential NCOs and officers were sent for training to the same depot. In 1948 the initial training was separated. After a few weeks training the potential officers had to appear before a Unit Selection Board (USB). This was often looked upon as something of a joke for if you came from a privileged background or had family connections the outcome was all but guaranteed. Those progressing from their USB interview now spent three days being assessed by a War Office Assessment Board. Here supposed initiative and leadership qualities were sought. Simple physical tests like crossing a river using planks or oil drums were undertaken. Giving a lecture for a few minutes on random subjects was also required. This gave an advantage to public school recruits as this requirement was practised at most leading establishments. Social confidence however mistaken was deemed essential.

Further interviews got to the heart of the matter. What was your background? School, father's occupation. Having a regional accent did not help. The Surrey stockbroker belt provided the most commissions of any county. Those from Wales appeared badly represented. Some regiments simply ignored the results of both intelligence and medical tests if the family was particularly well connected. Wealthy industrialists were frustrated that their sons remained in the ranks. For once money did not speak as loudly as breeding. Some obviously very bright recruits who did not quite fit the officer profile were moved to serve as sergeants, either in the education or intelligence corps. These were often young men who also had ideas or showed some independence of thought. Restless spirits with progessive ideas clearly needed to be hived off to a branch where they could spend the next couple of years doing something that was hopefully useful.

The most prestigious regiments had their own methods of recruiting. Whilst buying a commission was no longer possible the five Regiments of Foot, Guards and the Household Cavalry recruited their officers direct from school. The Grenadier Guards admitted that regimental headquarters kept files on potential officers, some of whom were put down for the regiment at birth. Interviews were carried out at Eton. Criticised for their elitist policy, they explained that the Guards spend much of their time in London. It was very expensive for a single junior officer without a private income so it deterred many from applying. Even Etonians were not guaranteed a place and were sometimes farmed out to lesser outfits like the Royal Artillery. That was just about acceptable, but they dreaded being consigned to the Royal Army Service Corps or maybe the Pioneer Corps. Perception in the officer ranks was everything. The arch snob Evelyn Waugh serving in the Grenadier Guards is quoted in his diary stating that he had cocktails with a group of proletarian officers at HQ.

Being a national service officer was in essence little different from being a prefect at school. Inspecting parades, over-seeing meals and dishing out punishments for minor misdemeanours. Life followed a similar pattern if posted abroad but all this changed on active service. Here officers and men were often thrown together. Some units were more democratic than others. Commandos trained together and relied on each other in dangerous situations. They often had to share the same tent and even drank together. Other regiments insisted on the strictest possible segregation. From extreme boredom, serving in Catterick or pretending to being busy in an RAF camp in Germany, the national service experience was as diverse as the people who undertook it. A chance for some to see the world and expand their previous horizons. For others it cemented their class prejudice, but the overall verdict was that the whole episode was a waste of time. And yet....perhaps all this is best recalled in the memories of Gerry Southworth, and here are his memories in his own words.

'The jury is still out on the usefulness of National Service. For many in my day it was a complete waste of time. Two years in a naval cookhouse in Portsmouth or two years pounding a typewriter in Aldershot must have been a very boring experience. Now over seventy years later I look back on my own service with thanks and even affection. Valuable lessons were learned and I saw places I never dreamed I would see. The total experience matured me at speed and has left me with indelible memories of places and people that have helped to shape my life.

'It was with joy and no apprehension when my papers arrived summoning me to serve for 'the duration of the present emergency', the initial training to be given by the King's Own Yorkshire Light Infantry (KOYLI). I had always wanted to join the Navy but if it had to be the Army, so be it, the KOYLI was my favourite regiment. By a curious coincidence my strongest school friend Jack had received identical instructions and we contrived to stay together for a good part of our service.

'The six weeks that followed everybody remembers. Intimidatory, tough, bullying, impossible tasks, instant punishments, all designed to create smart efficient soldiers, proud to wear the uniform and loyal to the regiment. Schoolboys rubbed shoulders with graduates, surveyors with labourers – in a rigid military structure it was a curious democratic experience. I revelled in it but the first unpleasant experience was soon to follow. Four of us, smart enough to uncover a petty theft culprit, were charged with mutiny! A night in the guardroom cell followed, giving us time to contemplate on the likely outcome, given that the punishment for mutiny at that time was the death sentence. The hearing next day was with the Commanding Officer who promptly gave us a reprieve and a lecture on the folly of taking the law into our own hands. LESSON ONE had been learned.

'Six weeks from our call-up we 'passed out' – our platoon outshone the others, we marched like guardsmen, could handle the rifle, the Sten gun and the Bren gun, were reasonable shots and were now trained killers. We could even garrotte!

'LESSON TWO was not short in coming. I had worn the KOYLI cap badge for one day only when the Army changed its mind and decided I should be in the Ordnance Corps, the custodian of the Army's arms and ammunition. A challenge was to come. As a Lance Corporal (one above a private soldier) I was judged to be senior enough to be in charge of a convoy of three civilian vehicles laden with ammunition at Easingwold in Yorkshire to be delivered to Woolwich Arsenal. The only soldier with three civilian drivers. All went well until half way down the Great North Road one of the three drivers announced that he had completed the lawful hours and could not proceed. My industrial relations skills (in use for the first time in my life) could not persuade him otherwise, and late in the evening I delivered two of the three to the Arsenal. 'Where's the third truck, my boy?' demanded the receiving Sergeant Major. 'You'll be for the high jump if he doesn't turn up tomorrow – he's probably delivered it to the IRA.' I contemplated his last remark and had a sleepless night. Fortunately all was well the following day, but the lesson was obvious and I didn't split any convoys in the dangerous territories to come.

'It's a long story but the Army had a series of mind changes and after my foolish rejection of the offer of WOSB (the selection board for Officer training - LESSON THREE), I joined Jack on a posting to Kenya. And even that changed. We found ourselves in Egypt, ostensibly to help the clearance of the Western Desert, left in a mess by Rommel and Montgomery. In reality it was to the Canal Zone, the Army's worst posting. Malaya, Trieste, Athens, Kenya all had their problems too, but some attractions as compensation. Egypt had none. Sandstorms, dust, mosquitoes, scorpions, typhoid, boredom and the hostility of the locals were to be the order of the day.

'I had to wait until the latter days of my service for my life to become really interesting and exciting. Having reached the dizzy heights of Sergeant I was entrusted to be in charge of a consignment of arms and ammunition on a Dakota DC3 for delivery to a desert airstrip called Mafraq in northern Transjordan. What journeys they were. I sat up front with the pilot and soon became an expert on the geography below. We would fly east to Aqaba and then due north, taking good care to be away from the Israeli border. Heavily into 'Seven Pillars of Wisdom' at that time I was able to get the pilot to fly low and investigate the very places on the infamous railway line that Lawrence had sabotaged so many years before. And of course Petra, 'rose red city, half as old as time' had to be investigated. More than once, with the enthusiasm and foolishness of youth, on our way back we would fly over the Negev, Israeli territory, to get back to a party in the Mess, risking an international incident. I have only learned in the last couple of years that four out of five Spitfires were shot down by the Israelis in the six months preceding our own incursions.

'The smile was taken off my face at the end of my service. Four of us, all sergeants, were languishing in a transit camp in Port Fuad awaiting a ship home for demobilisation. We were convinced that we had been forgotten as ship after ship came in but never a place for us. A swish ocean liner, the Georgic, homeward bound, came in from the far east and still no place for us. I was selected to raise our case officially, and I sought an interview with the Major in charge of movements. I complained bitterly that there had obviously been a mistake as personnel with higher demob numbers than ours were embarking. The Major glowered at me: 'the Army doesn't make mistakes – soldiers do. And it's nothing to do with demob numbers – you lot are in for the duration of the present emergency. So back to your tent and wait instructions.' I told the others what happened and there were no smiles.

'Not an hour later I received a message – get your kit and report to the Georgic – me but not the others. I commiserated with them, left and boarded. The speedy Georgic took forever to lumber around the

Mediterranean, Cyprus, Malta, Gibraltar and even Belfast so that the Royal Inniskillings could have a ceremonial welcome home. The end of my army service.

'By one of those rare coincidences I later met, in Sheffield of all places, one of the three I had left behind in the transit camp and enquired as to when did they eventually get home. 'About an hour after you left we were kitted out in civilian clothes, rushed to Cairo and flew that night, arriving home the following morning.' I still have a vision of a Major in Port Fuad still sucking his pipe with a self satisfied smile on his face.'

Was national service really a waste of time? Maybe, but in retrospect many appear quite nostalgic. A strange time of their life and one that is unlikely to be experienced by any future generation.

Chapter 27

Anniversary – A Postscript to the War

Most of us have heroes or role models we admire or aspire to emulate. This is particularly true when we are children. Then we often choose a film or sports star, although sometimes we pick someone closer to home. An older brother or sister whom we admire and are proud of. In the case of young Derek Twiddy it was his cousin Peter. A strongly built, good looking young man who was a keen sportsman and had done well at school. So well that rather than working in a factory or doing manual work like most working class kids he had secured a job as a clerk in a local office. Stockwell where Peter had been born and lived was a tough area. As a joke they often referred to it as Saint Ockwell which sounded much posher.

Back in war-time London families tended to live close to where they were born. The Twiddy family was based round Stockwell and Walthamstow with an outpost in Wood Green. Members of the extended family met each other regularly either for Sunday afternoon tea or a sing-song round the upright piano that dominated the Twiddys' parlour. It was through continual contact that young Derek got to know and admire his older cousin.

Peter Twiddy was born in Stockwell in 1921. He had a younger brother Eric who was also a great pal of Derek. Within a year of the outbreak of war Peter had enlisted in the RAF aged nineteen. It is obvious that the young man impressed for within two years he had achieved the rank of Sergeant in his role as an air gunner. He was proud to display a single-winged air crew badge with a wreath containing the letters AG signifying the dangerous job he undertook. The air gunner had to lie down in the freezing nose of the aircraft directing the pilot until the bombs were released over the target. The air gunner also trained as a reserve pilot, able to take over in an emergency.

After Mussolini entered the war it was decided that a member of the Special Operations Executive (SOE) should be sent to Albania to help organise resistance. The first attempt was short lived with the operative being captured, and it was April 1943 before a small group was established blowing up bridges and generally causing pockets of mayhem. On the night of 19th October 1943 a Halifax HR674 was allocated to carry out a special SOE operation named Sapling 7. The crew of seven were joined by Captain Alfred Careless and Signalman David Rockingham who were both attached to the SOE. The purpose of the trip was to drop much needed supplies as well as the two operatives who were due to join up with colleagues.

The aircraft took off from Tocra in Libya just before midnight. Unfortunately the aircraft never returned. Attempts were made to trace the aircraft, including searches of the sea but no trace was found. The drop zone had been high in the mountains above the village of Tragjas in Albania. A signal was received stating that the plane had crashed in the early hours of 20th October. It was assumed that the crash was more likely to have been due to engine failure rather than pilot error. Back home the family including Derek grieved, their sadness compounded by not knowing what really happened on that night all those years ago. The trail went cold and Peter's close relatives at the time were all dead before a series of investigations brought a remarkable closure to a seemingly forgotten tale of war.

It all started when a local Albanian farmer was ploughing his fields when he came across some bones and parts of a wrecked aircraft. Later a number of buckles from service kit was also found. The British Embassy was contacted and a team was deployed to investigate. An exact DNA match with Peter Twiddy's only surviving cousin confirmed that his whereabouts had been established after some seventy eight years. Peter had been killed on his twenty second birthday. In an extraordinary twist to his story he was finally laid to rest with full military honours on the very day that would have marked his one hundredth birthday had he survived. In a moving ceremony held at Tirana Park Memorial Cemetery in Albania attended by the Queen's Colour Squadron of the Royal Air Force. Perhaps the most fitting epitaph for Peter was spoken at the graveside: 'Sergeant Twiddy, on behalf of Her Majesty the Queen and all our armed forces, I salute you for your sacrifice.'

Chapter 28

Tinsel Time

During times of hardship it is always important to have something to look forward to. For children excitement about Christmas started weeks before the actual day. The first signs were signalled by schools rehearsing for a nativity play or the annual carol concert. Anticipation increased and hints were dropped about hoped for presents. After the war shop window displays became more inviting helped by being lit at night. Regent Street in London was packed in 1948 where for the first time since the war a spectacular display of Christmas decorations danced to a gentle breeze high above the heads of shoppers and tourists. The following year the Blackpool illuminations were restored. Switched on by the actress Anna Neagle, the illuminations again became a major tourist attraction.

As the decade drew to its end life was slowly dragging itself back to pre-war levels, but progress was so slow. Too slow for an impatient British public, but rationing and shortages persisted. Whilst the lights had gone on again in London and Blackpool there were few Christmas baubles available in the shops except the most basic paper chains. It was time to climb up into the loft again and drag down the boxes of rather moth eaten decorations kept from before the war. Tinsel that had long since lost it sparkle was draped over the Christmas tree and I remember a Father Christmas sitting in a very ancient biplane was given pride of place at the top of the tree. The few surviving baubles completed the rather sad tree decorations, although some rather bald paper bells did add a little colour.

Lesley Taylor was seven years old in 1949, and remembers that Christmas well. She lived with her parents and younger brother in a large house in Kirby Muxloe which had been requisitioned during the war. Her father was a manufacturer of nylon stockings, so by bartering with local farmers was able to offer a royal spread for Christmas lunch. On Christmas Eve the young child feigned sleep as her pillowcase bulging with presents was placed by her bed. Allowing time for her parents to go to sleep she very carefully unwrapped all her presents. By the morning all had been re-packaged so that her parents could enjoy her excitement at apparently seeing the gifts for the first time. She was obviously really impatient whilst other children might take all day unwrapping their goodies. Traits formed in childhood rarely change as the years pass.

It is reckoned that more marriages break down over the Christmas festivities than at any other time of the year. Certainly there is often tension as families are thrown together for the festivities. I remember feeling rather put out by being barred from our kitchen. My mum was cooking the lunch helped by her mother. There were peals of laughter and much banging of pots. Next door in the dining room my father's mother sat tutting and my father looked increasingly anxious. He was also being denied access to the kitchen. Eventually the door opened and red-faced and giggly they emerged. It was obvious that they were both tiddly. Teetotal granny looked sour and rather spoiled the meal as the tension rose. Two grandmothers, two extremes.

There was also tension at young Lesley Taylor's Christmas lunch. Surrounded by various uncles and aunts their meal was served by their resident cook and housekeeper. She was summoned to clear away plates and serve the next course by the ringing of a handbell. Brought up to always be polite to their cook the children were forbidden to ring the bell themselves and encouraged to help with the clearing away. The temptation of ringing the bell proved too much for her brother who rang it like a town crier. Banished to the hall the meal was ruined by the lad's cries of defiance as he kicked angrily at the skirting board.

Back in Edgware once the uneasy meal had been completed and the washing up done it was time for the arrival of relatives for afternoon tea. First came my smooth uncle Arthur with his bubbly blonde wife whom I adored. I had overheard my mum referring to her as 'no better than she ought to be' whatever that meant. I did not care as my glamorous aunt smothered me in kisses as she held me to her ample bosom. She always gave me a half crown whenever she visited. Unfortunately this was the last time as the marriage broke up soon after. The tension continued to increase with the next arrival. My father's sister was married to uncle Billy. Their arrival was welcomed with seeming reverence. The Daimler drew up outside and my father went to greet them. Uncle Billy looked like Fred Astaire and I could imagine him descending a grand staircase and taking Ginger Rogers in his arms. Instead he came up our garden path dressed in a grey suit and wearing spats to match. Billy was a director of Jays, the West End department store. To his face he was treated like royalty, but actually he was just a puffed up ego on legs.

Time now for the ritual Christmas games. Everyone joined in for 'hunt the parcel' but the favourite was 'consequences'. Bubbly aunt Pauline made a play for Billy who was obviously flattered and suddenly appeared quite human. Tea and cake were served and my mother breathed a sigh of relief as our strange relatives bid their farewells. Just time for a treat. My sister Ann and I were invited to sit in the Daimler and taken for a short spin. The car had headlamps the size of dinner plates and inside was the expensive smell of leather. Once round the block, we were back home and encouraged to almost genuflect our thanks to this rather ridiculous dapper little man.

There had been a gradual decline in church attendance since its height in Victorian Britain. Two wars had obviously tested the public's faith and the decline quickened except over Christmas where services tended to be packed. Older children were sometimes allowed to stay up for the traditional midnight service of carols and readings. Attendances at Catholic churches remained high with the Church of England experiencing the biggest falls. The churches serving the newly arrived West Indians were showing rapid growth with several churches being formed in Brixton within weeks of the arrival of the Windrush.

Christmas witnessed a strange levelling across society. From the very grandest to the most humble, most made an effort to put some sort of special spread on the table. The majority attempted to serve turkey or possibly a chicken. A favourite trick was to hang around a street market on Christmas Eve as the stallholder prepared to pack up for the day. Then they would off-load any produce unsold cheaply. With a turkey, chicken, goose or duck waiting to be carved, people across the country prepared to tuck in to a traditional Christmas lunch. Whilst James Lees-Milne prepared to open the last of his 1924 Krug, elsewhere it may have been a glass of brown ale or a sweet sherry that did the trick.

Winston Churchill writing to his wife Clementine, who was away travelling, reports on his Christmas in 1947. He informs her he has been 'most hospitably entertained by Mary and Christopher (his daughter and son-in-law) in their comfortable and pleasant farmhouse.' He continues,

'We spent a happy and peaceful Christmas Day and drank your health and Sarah's before we fell on the fat turkey.' Later he informs his wife that 'I took Edwina and Julian Sandys to the big circus at Olympia and they loved it.' Obviously enchanted by the young girl he continues, 'It was Edwina's ninth birthday. She is a very pretty little girl and may be a beauty one day I think.' This just underlines that even the great and the good enjoy the simple things in life which are available to all of us .

Meanwhile on the Welsh borders, Arthur Price-Jones' parents did their best to emulate the great man's enjoyment of that day, but fell somewhat short. For Arthur the presents he longed for never quite materialised. It was not through lack of trying on his father's part. Each year he beavered away making a selection of wooden toys, including a scooter. Regretfully still no bike. The Christmas decorations were sparse, but the one major concession made was the opening up of the 'posh' front room. A desultory fire failed to warm the room which remained chilly and damp as it was so rarely used. It did not take them long to return to the comfort of the cosy living room. Christmas lunch was only made remarkable by the excitement of Arthur and his brother trying the locate the sixpences hidden away in the pudding without breaking their teeth. With his parents both having 'signed the pledge', there was no alcohol to light the pud.

With the meal finished it was time for another Christmas ritual. Children across the land were told to be quiet, with no talking allowed. At three o'clock precisely the King started his annual address. It must have been an ordeal for him as the nation sat willing him to get his words out without stammering. His broadcast made in 1948 was typical in that he never said anything of consequence, but in these different times all listened intently. He referred with pride to his silver wedding and the arrival of his first grandson. Also of his sadness that ill health was preventing his intended tour of Australia and New Zealand. He went on to inform his subjects: 'Kingship is no isolated impersonal function, no abstract symbol of constitutional theory ......' On he droned, obviously trying to make a connection with his people, but his delivery was stiff and formal in words written for him and keeping his public at arm's length. No matter, the country listened before it was time for party games and afternoon tea.

In the Price-Jones family tea featured the serving of cold ham, courtesy of the pig club Arthur Price-Jones' father had contributed to throughout the year. They were joined by a favourite uncle and aunt who brought presents for the boys. Without children of their own the twin boys enjoyed a few hours of being spoilt. At nine o'clock it was off to bed and a return to a routine that seldom changed.

There were still two Christmas traditions that needed to be played out. For a six year old David Reynolds, Christmas Day was just a warm-up act to what he was really excited about - taking part in his first day's hunting. Before that his family's Christmas followed the pattern enjoyed across the country. His father was a farmer and landowner, a group who knew how to enjoy themselves. From mid-morning the drink flowed as friends and family made up a convivial Christmas luncheon party. Here too they all listened intently to the broadcast by the King before carrying on the celebrations. They were still in party spirit when David was finally packed off to bed. The next morning the young boy mounted his pony and joined other members of the Pytchley Hunt gathered at Hardingstone. It was a scene reproduced countless times on Christmas cards. The hunt was joined by a huge crowd of followers drinking mulled wine. Some of the horses were getting restless, pawing the ground, anxious to be on their way. Whilst there were people who did not approve of hunting, most country folk were very supportive and there was much shouting and cheering as the hounds set off with the riders in pursuit and not a protester in sight.

Hunting was an elite sport and expensive. As such it attracted the local aristocracy, landowners and wealthy farmers. The Pytchley Hunt had been in existence for over two hundred years and hunting was in young David's blood. Over the years he attended thousands of Meets. His uncle Ted had just about kept the hunt alive during the difficult war years. Eventually taking on the mantle, David became a very popular Master of Foxhounds.

Just when children thought that all the fun of Christmas had disappeared there was one final treat to be enjoyed. Pantomimes were produced all over the country, from leading theatres to village halls. In 1949 Jimmy Clitheroe was appearing in 'Cinderella' at the Bristol Hippodrome. The prestigious show at the London Palladium starred the Cockney comic Tommy Trinder in 'Puss in boots'. Pantomime originated in 16th century Italy but soon morphed into a uniquely British form, loud, raucous and rude.

Just entering the theatre was enough for many children to almost burst with excitement. The plush velvet seats, the illustrated programme and a live orchestra warming up in the pit beneath the stage. We never questioned why attractive young women were dressed as men, slapping their thighs and trying to looking masculine and failing, yet still so attractive to a young boy. There was music, laughter and endless slapstick. I remember a comic being pushed into a sort of tent and coming out as a row of sausages to screams of delight from all the children. It was bedlam. Perhaps the greatest treat was to be seated with your family in a box looking down directly on the stage. After all the curtain calls it was out to a dark, damp winter's evening and the realisation that the holiday was truly over and soon it would be back to school.

Chapter 29

Reflections and Moving On

There is often an attempt to capture the essence of a decade in a simple, all encompassing phrase. Hence the naughty nineties, the roaring twenties and the swinging sixties. They were all periods of excess and enjoyment. It is perhaps the lack of these which guarantees that for the 1940s no single phrase comes to mind.

Some who were youngsters at the start of the decade were now old enough to serve in the forces, get married and have children. Girls now old enough to seek their first job were not so well served with generally their options being limited. Nursing or secretarial work was about as high as most middle class girls aimed, whereas those from poorer backgrounds normally went to work in a local factory or possibly a position as a shop assistant. Now at least only a few went into service. A pointer to the future for women was the appointment of Helena Normanton and Rose Heilbron to become the first two female King's counsel.

Meanwhile another group of young ladies were preparing to 'come out'. All dressed in white indicating purity (not a state all could claim), they waited with their parents in the back of cars stretching down The Mall awaiting access to Buckingham Palace. Weighed down with the family jewels, the mothers were often more nervous than the young lady shortly to be presented, desperately hoping that their daughter would not fall over when curtseying to the sovereign. The ordeal over, it was time to party. A constant social whirl took place in the fashionable squares of Mayfair, Kensington or some ancient stately home. Fine settings then for meeting the right sort of chap with perhaps the possibility of joining two famous families. The cost of all this entertaining could be ruinous, but it was essential to keep up appearances whatever the cost.

Many matches were made each year with either titles or vast wealth being cemented. Some girls let the side down by running off to Gretna Green with a groom or a good looking footman, but mostly the young ladies played by the accepted rules. Some resented this marriage market, but to be left without any takers was a source of great distress for mothers of even the plainest of girls.

The London season remained in place for at least a few years yet, but was life going to improve for the less privileged? The dystopian novel '1984' by George Orwell suggested that within thirty five years Britain would become a police state with big brother watching our every move. Copies of the book flew off the shelves. It was a great story but the country had suffered enough. Life was going to get better.

Rather than see an improvement, in June 1949 the government was forced to devalue the pound from $4.03 to $2.80 in an attempt to help our flagging exports. This also had the effect of making imports more expensive and a rise in the cost of living. Austerity continued to hold us in its unwelcome embrace.

There were a few more encouraging pointers. The first commercial flight of the Comet was heralded as a triumph for British technology. A short lived claim as design faults began to appear. However it did give a glimpse of the potential for future air travel. On a more mundane level the first opening of a public launderette was welcomed by thousands of housewives. Many youngsters accompanied their mothers and sat watching the weekly wash spinning hypnotically in front of them. With money still tight for most, the abolition of clothes rationing did not lead to an instant rush to the stores. At least not to buy, but window shopping became a national pastime and Butterick dress patterns offered women the chance to run up the latest Paris fashions within a few weeks of their appearance on the cat-walk. Suddenly we were a nation of dressmakers.

Children were also offered a little cheer as sweet rationing was abolished. Bulls-eyes, sherbet drops, toffees and liquorice sticks were sucked, licked and swallowed in huge quantities, followed by a trip to the dentist as an entire generation had their mouths filled with amalgam. Seemingly, as ever in post-war Britain, it was a case of one step forward, one step back.

Change tends to be more noticeable in urban areas rather than in the country, but down in deepest Wiltshire something was stirring which was going to set a trend amongst some of the largest landowners in Britain. The Marquis of Bath decided to open his Longleat House to the public. Shock, horror was the initial reaction from some. It was a gamble but the Marquis was proved right. We are all a little nosy and none more so than the British public. What was it really like hidden away behind those impressive gates? Soon thousands were finding out and roaming the gardens having paid their half a crown entrance money. A cafe and a gift shop were opened. Perhaps without really understanding the impact his venture was to make, the Marquis had started a new uniquely British industry, one which was swiftly followed by other blue-bloods.

Whilst the Longleat experiment emphasised the changes slowly happening in British society, the 'Last Night Of The Proms' represented the traditions that were a source of pride to so many Britons. Held in mid September 1949 at the Royal Albert Hall, it was a chance to indulge in a little national self-congratulation with a raucous rendering of 'Land of hope and glory'. Today the lyrics of Arthur Benson to the music of Edward Elgar is considered by some to be too xenophobic. Over seventy years ago few had such qualms as the soprano Jean Howe led the singing.

What is the consensus of those who grew up during the difficult war years and the austerity that followed? Certainly they have witnessed more changes that any previous generation. That skinny army are now old and many are frail. They have probably witnessed more changes during their lifetime than any other generation. They were probably too young to appreciate many of the most important events then that continue to affect our lives today. The forming of the National Health Service was a radical idea set in motion by Nye Bevan, and initially praised across much of the world. From its inception the costs started to get out of control. Even today it is an insatiable beast as its overworked staff attempt to deal with an ever growing tide caused in part by people living longer.

The explosion of the atomic bomb over Hiroshima had on-going implications for us all. Was the world now a safer or more dangerous place? It was assumed that no country would be mad enough to start a nuclear conflict, but the Cuban crisis tested nerves and even today there are worries as world tensions increase again.

The arrival of the Windrush was the first indication that Britain was about to change forever with the arrival of former members of the Commonwealth to form the basis of today's multi-racial society. There have been no 'rivers of blood' as predicted by Enoch Powell. Just as with our relationship with the Americans during the war had been initially difficult, so it was with these new arrivals as gradually British suspicion of others began to subside as our new diversity became part of our everyday lives.

As the 1940s drew to a close there were still wars being fought in Palestine, but as youngsters we looked forward to what life could throw at us. Can we remember waking up on a sunny morning during our school holidays with no pressing worries other than going out to play? That sense of innocence does not last long, yet on such a morning whether we lived in an inner city or out in the sticks, the feeling of excitement and anticipation is unique to the young before the stresses and worries of adult life arrive.

The skinny army of the 1940s now form an ageing tribe whose underlying optimism and spirit remains. In true war-time character they plan to 'keep calm and carry on'.

Appendix

Some Well Known Children of the 1940s –
A Decade of the Talents

Sir Alan Ayckbourn
Jane Asher
Dame Shirley Bassey
Jane Birkin
Tony Blackburn
Sir Michael Caine
Sir Bobby Charlton
Brian Cox
Baron Ken Clarke of Nottingham
Eric Clapton
Dame Judy Dench
Marianne Faithfull
Graeme Garden
David Hemmings
John Humphrys
Sir Geoff Hurst
Sir Derek Jacobi
Sir Mick Jagger
Sir David Jason
Sir Elton John
Sir Tom Jones

Neil Kinnock
Joanna Lumley
Miriam Margolyes
Sir Paul McCartney
Sir Ian McKellen
Dame Helen Mirren
Mitch Murray CBE
Pete Murray
Sir Van Morrison
Michael Palin
Charlotte Rampling
Lynn Redgrave
Charles Saatchi
John Simpson
Jon Snow
Sir Ringo Starr
Patrick Stewart
Sir Rod Stewart
Sir Tom Stoppard
David Warner

Bibliography

Bishop, Patrick, *Fighter Boys* (Harper Collins, 2008)

Brown, Mike, *The Wartime House* (Sutton Publishing, 2001)

Brown, Mike, *Wartime Broadcasting* (Shire Publishing, 2018)

Donovan, Paul, *The Radio Companion* (HarperCollins, 1991)

Foster, Andy, *Radio comedy 1938–68* (Virgin Books, 1996)

Gardiner, Juliet, *Wartime: Britain 1939–1945* (Headline, 2004)

Hampton, Janie, *The Austerity Olympics* (Aurum Press, 2008)

Hopkins, Harry, *The New Look: A Social History of the Forties and Fifties in Britain* (Secker and Warburg, 1964)

Jackson, Alan, *London's Metroland* (Capital History, 2006)

Laver, James, *Costume and Fashion* (Thames and Hudson, 1969)

Kynaston, David, *Austerity Britain 1945–51* (Bloomsbury Publishing, 2007)

Marr Andrew, *A History of Modern Britain* (Pan Macmillan UK Books, 2008)

Moynaham, Brian, *The British Century* (Random House, 1997)

van Oppen, Martin, *Embers of Empire* (Matador, 2014)

Soames, Mary, *Speaking for Themselves: The Personal Letters of Winston and Clementine Churchill* (Doubleday, 1998)

Waugh, Evelyn, *The Diaries of Evelyn Waugh* (Penguin Books, 2002)

Wilson, Elizabeth, *Through the Looking Glass* (BBC Books, 1989)

Ziegler, Philip, *London at War, 1939–1945* (Pimlico, 2002)

Index